Commentary on Old Testament Stories

Roy Wilkinson

RSCP

The publisher is grateful for the encouragement and support of Robert Dulaney in making this new edition possible.

The name Waldorf really belongs only to the first school of its type, the one founded by Rudolf Steiner in Stuttgart, Germany for the children of the workers at the Waldorf-Astoria factory. It has since been adopted as the generic name of schools conducted according to Rudolf Steiner's recommendations. In place of Waldorf some establishments call themselves Rudolf Steiner schools. Others take a distinctive name and add Waldorf or Rudolf Steiner in some connection as a subtitle.

ISBN 0-945803-57-5

Book orders may be made through Rudolf Steiner College Bookstore. Tel. 916-961-8729, FAX 916-961-3032.

Rudolf Steiner College Press
9200 Fair Oaks Boulevard
Fair Oaks, CA 95628, USA

Contents

About the Author

Roy Wilkinson has been connected with the work of Rudolf Steiner for over 60 years. Born in Leicestershire, England, he was educated both locally and in Switzerland. He attended the Goetheanum School of Speech and Drama, receiving his certificate from Frau Dr. Steiner herself.

After working at an educational center, he made excursions into the fields of medicine (with Weleda) and agriculture, and eventually became a teacher. Over some forty years he taught in Steiner and state schools in England, Germany, and Switzerland. He has also taught children in need of special care.

Mr. Wilkinson has been active as an advisor to schools and lecturer on Rudolf Steiner education and Anthroposophy in many European countries, in South America as well as in English-speaking countries.

Another major contribution is the writing he has done over a period of more than twenty years. Wilkinson has produced introductory books on Rudolf Steiner education and its philosophical foundations. These and his curriculum guide booklets have been highly appreciated by teachers, parents, and those seeking answers to personal questions. A complete list of current editions is at the end of this volume.

Foreword

The Bible is the most widely read book in the world, the most widely distributed and the most translated. Probably more books have been written about the Bible than any other single subject. The word Bible itself means The Book. It is quoted endlessly. It is a collection of documents from various sources and from various languages. Both Old and New Testaments contain wonderful descriptions and stories which appear very strange. This is not surprising considering the nature of the matter with which they deal. There is, however, an additional complication in trying to understand the Old Testament because of its history.

It is generally assumed that much of the contents of the Old Testament was passed down orally. The time at which the books were actually written is a matter of conjecture although it is known that great activity in this respect took place during and after the Babylonian captivity. With the exception of a small part of the Book of Daniel and several other small passages, the original scripts were in Hebrew, a language which has no vowels in its alphabet. Hence, to the reader, a word might have several meanings, any of which might be valid. There is also no certainty as to the authors. The first five books of the Old Testament are ascribed to Moses, yet he can hardly have described his own death. A book may bear the name of a particular prophet but that is no guarantee that he wrote it. It may contain a third person's account. Some books appear to have had more than one author. Furthermore, the mentality and customs of the writers were very different from those of today.

We, in the English version, have translations from translations and it would take a bold man, or a foolish one, to assert that every word, as written, is divinely inspired. Divine inspiration may well apply to the original Hebrew. Translators may also be inspired but in time translations become less reliable. Of the forty-seven translators who worked on the King James version of the Bible, which is in common use in the English-speaking world, only three were Hebrew scholars and two of these died before the work was finished. Moreover, they were instructed that the new translation should not basically contradict any belief then held. Luther, the father of Protestantism in Germany, translated from a Latin text.

Taking the Bible stories as they are, there are obvious discrepancies and events which would strain the mind of the most credulous. In the story of the creation the light is created on the first day but sun, moon and stars only on the fourth. Obviously, statements are not quite what they seem. Are we to believe such a fantastic story as that of Samson killing three thousand Philistines with the jawbone of an ass?

Yet the stories are undoubtedly true—in a sense. They are true in the sense that fairy stories and mythologies are true. The knight overcoming the dragon shows the conquest of good over evil. Odysseus in his wanderings demonstrates an inner path of development. These are truths in imaginative pictures. Children have an imaginative understanding and so had people of earlier times when powers of intellect were less developed. Fairy stories, myths, the Old Testament stories, go back to these times. They can be appreciated in their own way but today's rational mind is inclined to dismiss their content as fantasies. Yet most of such stories are based on spiritual facts and in modern times spiritual facts are only accessible to the few. One of the few was Rudolf Steiner. With his faculty of spiritual vision and his ability to investigate worlds beyond the physical, Rudolf Steiner founded a spiritual science to which he gave the name Anthroposophy. With the aid of such a science it is possible to appreciate the Bible in a rational way.

Some of the events depicted are purely symbolical; others are of a verifiable historical nature but at the same time can also be interpreted symbolically.

As a teacher, the author's original intention was to rewrite the Old Testament stories for children but it was soon apparent that, to do this, a somewhat protracted and arduous study would be necessary. This book is the result of that study.

In an education which takes real notice of child development there is a particular place for the Old Testament stories. At the age of ten, children are leaving the airy-fairy world of infancy and are becoming much more interested in things of the earth. They begin, at the same time, to feel their own individuality, thus confirming, albeit unconsciously, their inner growth. Children receive pictures into their souls, and these provide spiritual nourishment.

Earth history is bound up with cosmic history. Only in the course of time does the earth become a separate unit and even then it is still influenced by the cosmos. The Old Testament leads from prehistoric to historic times, from a description of a divine creation to trials and tribulations in the physical world and the advent of a Saviour. Names like Adam and Noah are not historical but symbolic; only later do we meet historical personalities.

The progress of human development parallels that of the earth. Humanity, created in spiritual heights, enters the material world and strives towards independence. Every human being follows a similar path but the story of human creation in Genesis is not concerned with the primeval origin but with the origin of the earthly human being. The name Adam actually means 'earth human being.'

With Abraham the story of the Israelites begins but the story of the Israelites is also the story of human development. The Patriarchs have a certain clairvoyance which is fading. Esau and Jacob represent the dissolution of the old order and the coming of the new. Jacob has a new consciousness. The Moses episode illustrates the transition from being God-directed to having independent judgement and self-consciousness. With the kings comes a more human element. A dynasty is created through inheritance and not through divine guidance. Solomon shows a peak in worldliness. The prophets point to the coming of Christ, which, in human development, is paralleled by the birth of the ego.

The following notes are intended to be elucidations of the Old Testament stories in the light of Rudolf Steiner's spiritual science.

With the exception of the Creation, where the actual Biblical text is used, a summary of each story is given, followed by indications of its background significance. It must not be concluded, however, that such explanation as is offered is the only one. The author writes as a student and not as an authority. Where a direct interpretation from Dr. Steiner or other source is given, this is stated. Where there are particular problems in finding a satisfactory explanation, this is also indicated.

It is obvious that much of what is contained here will be better understood after an intensive study of Anthroposophy.

Earth: Its Creators and First Inhabitants

From the creation of the earth to its consolidation

In the beginning God created the heaven and the earth.
And the earth was without form, and void;
and darkness was upon the face of the deep.

THE SEVEN DAYS OF CREATION

The Biblical story of creation is couched in magnificent language which everyone can appreciate. To understand what is implied is not so easy. Fortunately, Rudolf Steiner has given an account of evolution from the spiritual scientific aspect and this, although complicated, clarifies the matter considerably. He describes three so-called planetary conditions of the earth. The first is a huge globe of heat, a manifestation of spiritual beings, in which our whole solar system was included as undifferentiated mass. There was a development from the heat element into a sort of gaseous substance and light. At a third stage there was a condensation to liquid.

These older stages must not be thought of as in any way physical and the events are not such as would be experienced in present conditions. The language used, therefore, can only be approximate. One has to think of the elements (heat, gas, light, liquid) in the sense of prototypes, not as we understand them. Perhaps the nearest that we can get with our mortal understanding is to think of them as spiritual ancestors.

In giving these descriptions there is another factor to be borne in mind, namely, time. Whereas we think of time as offering a sort of sequence, time, in our sense, did not exist before the advent of the solar system, which was a later development.

The three planetary conditions are known as Ancient Saturn, Ancient Sun and Ancient Moon. They are connected with our present Saturn, Sun and Moon but not identical. After Ancient Moon, begins the development of the Earth. (Written with a capital E, *Earth* refers to a planetary body in which the present sun, moon, planets and our earth were still united. They separated and, in the separation, our earth—small *e*—came into existence.)

It is the general rule in evolution that, before anything new can develop, there is a recapitulation of former conditions. Thus, when Ancient Sun comes into existence, there is a recapitulation of Ancient Saturn; when Ancient Moon is formed, there is a recapitulation of Ancient Saturn and Ancient Sun. At the beginning of Earth development there was a recapitulation of all the former planetary stages.

After Ancient Moon there emerges the cosmic body Earth, and in its development we differentiate various stages. These are: Polaris, Hyperborea, Lemuria, Atlantis, then post-Atlantis, which is the earth as we know it at present. Polaris, Hyperborea, Lemuria are recapitulations respectively of Ancient Saturn, Ancient Sun and Ancient Moon. Atlantis is new. At the beginning of Earth development (Polaris) sun, moon, earth and planets form one body and in due course become independent units although still interactive.

In the evolution of the earth we have to think of a gradual densification or consolidation. To begin with, and without delving too deeply into the niceties of philosophy, the process might be likened to an idea which becomes reality. But the ideas in creation were the thoughts of the gods which, in time, were clothed with physical reality— "frozen thoughts"—to use Emerson's expression. This applies equally to the human being and to the earth. The human being existed spiritually as a thought of the gods long before appearing physically.

In the Polaris stage of Earth development the solar system begins to take shape. Polaris consisted of a mixture of warmth, gaseous and fluid substance, but again it must be emphasised that it was spiritual substance, however contradictory the term may appear. If we can consider our thoughts as spiritual substance, then this spiritual substance referred to is the thoughts, the brooding, the musing of higher beings. They are recollecting or summarising within their souls the earlier states of planetary existence; but this divine musing is creative and it germinates productively. The opening words of Genesis refer to this.

First there is a mixture of the substances, then the finer gaseous element separates out, becoming eventually our present sun and radiating its influence to the earth from outside. At a later stage the moon, our present moon, leaves, and what is left becomes earth. In speaking of sun and moon it must also be borne in mind that we are dealing with spiritual beings whose home or manifestation is in the heavenly bodies.

The first words of Genesis refer then to the recapitulation of the ancient planetary conditions at the beginning of Earth evolution (Polaris—recapitulation of Ancient Saturn) and to the time when the sun parted from the sun/moon/earth mass in Hyperborea (recapitulation of Ancient Sun.) Most of the creation story, then, takes place in Lemuria (recapitulation of Ancient Moon).

In the beginning

This refers to the beginning of Earth evolution which resulted in the present solar system. At this stage there is an interweaving of the elemental substances of heat, gas and liquid which are really the embodiment or means of expression of spiritual beings.

God

The word in the original Hebrew is Elohim. It is a plural and the Elohim are high ranking spiritual beings, called in Greek the Exusiai, or by other designation, Spirits of Form. God as a collective term is justified insofar as the Elohim work as a group, combining their individual talents with the aim of creating the human being. They live and weave in the prototype elements of heat, gas and liquid.

created

The Elohim are engaged in productive musing. What lives in their souls becomes real.

the heaven and the earth.

In their musing the Elohim recall and recapitulate the events when the warmth of Ancient Saturn divided into light and gaseous substance and Ancient Sun was born. In their minds was the idea of something manifesting outwardly, connected with the light, and something with inner activity, connected with the denser element. These two focal points are described as heaven and earth but they also refer to the potential human being, a being of heaven and earth, of soul and body. The Elohim are calling forth an image of the human being.

And the earth was without form, and void;

Void means 'empty' but the earth was only empty and without form insofar as the spiritual substance was not tangible. There was an interweaving of spiritual beings. The Hebrew refers to "creative chaos."

and darkness was upon the face of the deep.

In evolution there is progression and retardation. Some beings advance and some remain behind. When Ancient Saturn was transformed, some beings progressed in their development, some lagged behind. Here the Elohim are recollecting the backward spirits which they experience as darkness.

And the Spirit of God moved upon the face of the waters.

By *waters* is meant the mixture of elements. The Elohim are becoming more active.

(The Bible narrative so far refers to events taking place in the Polaris Epoch.)

And God said, "Let there be light": and there was light.

The Elohim recollect, or re-form, or recapitulate within their own souls the transformation which took place when Ancient Saturn dissolved into light and gaseous substance. These elements united again but the separation was restaged in Hyperborea when certain beings of light moved out into the cosmos and formed a new abode which eventually became what we see as the sun. Other beings originated planets.

And God saw the light, that it was good and God divided the light from the darkness.

The Elohim became aware of what was being produced and the gaseous substance manifested as darkness.

And God called the light Day, and the darkness he called Night. And the evening and the morning were the first day.

When one set of spirits is ruling, there is the experience of light. The existence of backward beings was already mentioned. When they rule, it is night. The original does not use the word *night* in the modern sense but it refers to members of the Archai (Spirits of Time) who had remained backward in their development. What is translated as *day* refers to a member of the Archai who has followed a normal development. The Elohim appointed two sets of spirits to work in the interests of human existence, which is an interplay of expansion and contraction.

And God said, Let there be a firmament in the midst of the waters, and let it divide the waters from the waters.
And God made the firmament, and divided the waters which were under the firmament from the waters which were above the firmament, and it was so.
And God called the firmament Heaven. And the evening and the morning were the second day.

When the Ancient Sun gave way to the Ancient Moon, the gaseous substance condensed to a sort of liquid but the liquid had two forms. One was a cloud-like airy vapour, the other denser and heavy. Between what was above and what was below was the firmament. That which rose was connected with the light element and called Heaven; the opposite pole was of an earth nature. In what expands upwards is a recapitulation of Ancient Sun or its counterpart, Hyperborea, at the beginning of the Lemurian Epoch. The denser liquid conditions refer to Lemuria, the recapitulation of Ancient Moon. *Second day* means the appointment of subordinate spirits.

And God said, Let the waters under heaven be gathered together unto one place, and let the dry land appear, and it was so.
And God called the dry land Earth; and the gathering together of the waters called he Seas; and God saw that it was good.
And God said, Let the earth bring forth grass, the herb yielding seed, and the fruit tree yielding fruit after his kind, whose seed is in itself, upon the earth: and it was so.
And the earth brought forth grass, and herb yielding seed after his kind, and the tree yielding fruit, whose seed was in itself, after his kind: and God saw that it was good.
And the evening and the morning were the third day.

The watery element from Ancient Moon was recapitulated but further densified and now land, albeit without definite contours, began to crystallise from the liquid. This was a new development.

The sun forces, that is, the sun beings who were now free of the moon/earth, began to radiate into the new element. In Ancient Sun, spiritual beings had incorporated etheric forces into the existing mass, and this then is a recapitulation of their activity in the new element. As yet, however, the individual plants do not appear. What is here present are the group-souls of the plants, the species (after their kind). In the minds of the Elohim is the picture of plant existence as it had been on Ancient Sun now reappearing in the new element of land.

Again servants were appointed.

In the Ancient Moon there had been a division of forces. Two spheres had formed from the one as a result of two groups of beings requiring different conditions. Eventually the two spheres united. Lemuria is basically a recapitulation of Ancient Moon.

It is not stated in the Bible that during this period the earth/moon mass separated into the two units. However, according to Dr. Steiner, the hardening forces in the combined body were getting too powerful. Certain spiritual beings took it upon themselves, therefore, to remove them. The result of this was the formation of the present moon. It was a process which took place over immense periods of time.

And God said, Let there be lights in the firmament of the heaven to divide the day from the night; and let them be for signs, and for seasons, and for days, and for years:
And let them be for lights in the firmament of the heaven to give light upon the earth: and it was so.
And God made two great lights; the greater light to rule the day and the lesser light to rule the night: he made the stars also.
And God set them in the firmament of the heaven to give light upon the earth.
And to rule over the day and over the night, and to divide the light from the darkness: and God saw that it was good.
And the evening and the morning were the fourth day.

This is not to be understood as original creation on the fourth so-called *day*. In Hyperborea sun and planets had parted from the general mass and had become distinct entities. Moon and earth are now also separate units. Now that the earth is, so to speak, free of these forces within it, they begin to affect it from outside. Let us not forget that the heavenly bodies are really the vehicles of spiritual beings.

The *lights for signs* mean that the Elohim assigned beings to take care of earthly rhythms. Those concerned are known as the Spirits of Time.

And God said, Let the waters bring forth abundantly the moving creature that hath life, and fowl that may fly above the earth in the open firmament of heaven.
And God created great whales, and every living creature that moveth, which the waters brought forth abundantly, after their kind, and every winged fowl after his kind: and God saw that it was good.
And God blessed them, saying, Be fruitful and multiply, and fill the waters in the seas, and let fowl multiply in the earth.
And the evening and the morning were the fifth day.

On Ancient Moon a new kingdom was added to that of plant and mineral, namely, animality. When the recapitulation of Ancient Moon took place during the Lemurian Epoch of earth development, the astral forces flowed into the new conditions of air and water, bringing into existence the group-souls of the creatures of the water and the air. By the so-called *fifth day* all the recapitulations had taken place.

And God said, Let the earth bring forth the living creature after his kind, cattle, and creeping thing, and beast of the earth after his kind:, and it was so.
And God made the beast of the earth after his kind, and cattle after their kind, and every thing that creepeth upon the earth after his kind: and God saw that it was good.
And God said, Let us makeman in our image, after our likeness: and let them have dominion over the fish of the sea, and over the fowl of the air, and over the cattle, and over all the earth, and over every creeping thing that creepeth upon the earth.
So God created man in his own image, in the image of God created he him: male and female created he them. . . .
And the evening and the morning were the sixth day.

The earth conditions were now balanced and real earth existence could begin. The group-souls began to manifest in the individual animals on earth but the forms were still flexible.

In the Biblical account human beings come into existence on the sixth day, yet from other sources, we learn that, potentially, they existed already.

The fact that human beings are first mentioned on the sixth day and then again later (created from the dust of the earth) must be taken to indicate stages of development. The human being existed first in spirit, in the bosom of the Elohim. In the previous planetary conditions, vehicles for the human spirit were created by higher beings but these vehicles did not exist in the form we understand them at present. If they are designated physical body, etheric, astral, it is not in the modern sense but as prototypes. Even then, as evolution proceeds, there is continual change and modification. Up to the sixth day the human being did not appear in the physical and that was not physical as the term is used today. "Let us make man" signifies that the Elohim have reached a definite state in their activity. Their human being has the beginnings of physicality. "Male and female created he him" should read: "Male/female created hehim." Human beings were bi-sexual.

Thus the heavens and the earth were finished, and all the host of them.
And on the seventh day God ended his work which he had made; and he rested on the seventh day from all his work which he had made.

At first the Elohim worked together as individuals with a common goal. Now there was a change and in the next passage we note a new expression for the divinity, the Lord God.

Six of the Elohim now gave up a portion of their being to the seventh that he might continue their work. The six, to a great extent, turned their attention elsewhere. This is the significance of the Sabbath, the day of rest.

The totality of the Elohim is called God. The Lord God is the appointed seventh and is properly named as Jehovah Elohim.

These are the generations of the heavens and of the earth when they were created, in the day that the Lord God made the earth and the heavens.
And every plant of the field before it was in the earth, and every herb of the field before it grew:

It is difficult to make much of this passage unless we take Dr. Steiner's rendering which is: "What is referred to in the following verses is the offspring of the heavenly and earthly beings, created by the Elohim and further developed by Jehovah Elohim."

for the Lord God had not caused it to rain upon the earth, and there was not a man to till the ground.
But there went up a mist from the earth, and watered the whole face of the ground.

The conditions on the earth were changing but there was still no ground which could be cultivated. The human being was not yet in material form on a material earth.

And the Lord God formed man of the dust of the ground, and breathed into the nostrils the breath of life; and man became a living soul.

The six Elohim had withdrawn, leaving their representative, Jehovah Elohim, to continue further with their idea of creating an earthly being. The moon had separated from the earth but moon forces, whose nature is death, were left in the earth. These are referred to as *dust*. When Jehovah Elohim forms a human being of the dust of the ground, he is endowing the Elohim human being with consolidating forces. With the breath of life the spirit of the human being becomes housed in the vehicles prepared over long periods. It is a pre-condition of ego-consciousness.

And the Lord God planted a garden eastward in Eden; and there he put the man whom he had formed. . . .
And the Lord God commanded the man, saying, Of every tree of the garden thou mayest freely eat:
But of the tree of the knowledge of good and evil, thou shalt not eat of it: for in the day that thou eatest thereof thou shalt surely die.

We have already noted that when the creation of the human being on the sixth day is mentioned, this is not really a creation but a stage of development. Similarly when the planting of a garden is recorded, it is also a staging post. It represents a development of human consciousness.

The Garden of Eden is Paradise, the spiritual world; but even in the spiritual world there are different regions and different states of consciousness. The human being now has the beginnings of a feeling of self-consciousness and a changing mode of perception. Eating of the forbidden fruit is a symbol for acquiring knowledge. The consequences of such an act are pointed out. With knowledge comes freedom to choose. As dying in this world is an awakening in the spiritual, so dying in the spiritual is an awakening in the physical.

And out of the ground the Lord God formed every beast of the field, and every fowl of the air; and brought them unto Adam to see what he would call them:

Suddenly the name Adam appears. *Adam* means 'Earth Human Being.' The passage should therefore read: the Lord God formed every beast, etc. and brought them unto the Earth Human Being to see what name they would receive.

Mention of Earth Human Being emphasises the direction of evolution. The naming of animals is a further sign of growing self-consciousness. Only in the recognition of self as distinct from the world outside does self-consciousness arise. Naming the animals means recognising them, recognising them as something distinct from the self. These events foreshadow the Fall.

***And the rib, which the Lord God had taken from man, made he a woman* (Eve).**

The narrative describes a stage of completion. The picture, however, is difficult to understand. It may have come about through a mistranslation, The word for *rib* in Hebrew also means 'side'. This passage could therefore mean that the Lord God took one side (i.e. one characteristic) of the Earth Human Being for special development. That is, different characteristics were developed in Earth humans, resulting in male and female, man and woman.

When the moon and the earth separated on the so-called *third day,* certain processes connected with fructification had to change. The earlier method of reproduction was that when related souls approached from the spiritual worlds, the human beings gave of their own etheric substance, into which such souls could incarnate. Human beings were hermaphrodites. Actual sexual union only took place at a far later stage but as a preliminary two distinct types of human being made their appearance. There were those with a strong imaginative faculty and others with a strong will element. The forces within the soul moulded the still plastic physical and eventually the two sexes came into being.

The story of the Fall also describes the completion of events which had begun much earlier.

There had been certain beings in the spiritual world who had failed in their normal progress and they had become self-willed. They are known as Luciferic beings. Ever since human beings had been endowed with astrality, i.e. the possibility of having feelings, passions, desires, they were open to Luciferic influence. For their own purposes these beings made humans aware of themselves earlier than planned by the creators; they awakened the senses of humans (opened their eyes) who began to lose consciousness of the divine in favour of the terrestrial. By becoming conscious of themselves in the world of the senses, they acquired the ability to choose freely between good and evil.

For the earth in general the Luciferic influence brought about a condensation to solid and fluid. A physical, material world came into being and humans acquired physical bodies. They came down from the periphery to an earth which was becoming firm and solid. Life in the physical world brings with it "work in the sweat of thy face" and the pain of childbearing, in other words, toil, travail and affliction.

NOTE ON THE NAMES OF THE DIVINITY

In the main the divinity is referred to by three different names: God, the Lord God, the Lord. In the Hebrew the equivalents are: Elohim, Jehovah Elohim, Jehovah. The connection between the Elohim and Jehovah has already been explained. In the Biblical records it is a matter of consciousness. The world and the spiritual human beings, also the recreation of the earth after the flood, are the work of the Elohim. Jehovah Elohim is concerned with earthly human beings. Human consciousness, however, did not remain in the spiritual heights and Jehovah, without the designation of Elohim, came to be looked upon by the Jews as their god and father-creator of the world.

CAIN AND ABEL

Cain and Abel were the sons of Adam and Eve. Of Cain, Eve said, "I have gotten a man from the Lord." Cain was a tiller of the ground; Abel, a shepherd. They brought offerings to the Lord. Cain brought the fruit of the ground; Abel, the firstlings of his flock. Cain's offering was rejected. He showed his annoyance and the Lord reprimanded him, telling him that he must master the ever-present temptation to do wrong. Cain met his brother in the field and slew him.

The Lord questioned Cain about the event but obtained little response, merely the words: "Am I my brother's keeper?" Then the Lord explained to Cain that he had brought a curse upon himself, that he would henceforward be a fugitive and a vagabond upon the earth and that when he tilled the ground, it would no longer yield him its fertility. Cain realised his misdeed and feared that anyone finding him would slay him, but the Lord put a mark on him saying that no one must harm him under pain of attracting sevenfold vengeance.

Cain left the country with his wife and in their new dwelling place they had a son whom they called Enoch. Cain built a city and named it with his son's name, Enoch. Their descendants became builders of cities and of musical instruments, agriculturalists, artists and artisans.

Another son, Seth, was born to Adam and Eve. Eve looked upon him as a replacement for Abel. Legends say that Seth took a pilgrimage to find Paradise and that Adam bequeathed to him the Holy Book of Wisdom. His descendants became sages and priests.

NOTES

The story of Cain and Abel comes immediately after that of the expulsion from Paradise. Earth is still in its Lemurian state. It is a period of change where old conditions give way to new. Cain and Abel are representatives of humanity at the time of this change. The fact that they bring offerings and "began to call upon the name of the Lord" shows that divine guidance is receding. Individual traits are becoming apparent.

Cain has an attitude which belongs to the past. He has to bring about a transformation of his being. His descendants become actively engaged in the material world. Abel (or Seth, taking the legend into consideration) is concerned with the cherishing and cultivation of wisdom.

The point of the story is that humanity will no longer be under divine guidance but is taking the step towards self-responsibility. This means that faculties which the human being possessed at one stage must be metamorphosed and redeployed.

In the note on the seventh day it was already pointed out that where the word God is used, it refers to the Elohim. The Lord God is Jehovah Elohim, the member of the hierarchy of the Elohim on whom devolved especially the task of furthering earth development. Now we are confronted with a third expression for the divinity, the Lord. In the Hebrew this is Jehovah.

Cain, tiller of the ground

When Eve says she has gotten a man from the Lord, this must be taken to imply that Cain has some special connection with the divine. His offering is "fruit of the ground," i.e., from the plant world, the innocent realm of Paradise. We also note that Cain speaks with the Lord. From these facts we may deduce that he lives in a pre-Fall state of consciousness. Yet something new is stirring within him. Since there was no firm earth in Lemuria, "fruit of the ground" and "tiller of the ground" must have different connotations. "Tiller of the ground" means one who has creative activity, initiative, enterprise. "Fruit of the ground" can only mean that Cain offers something outdated. This is the reason why his offering is rejected.

The Lord tells him he has no reason to be cross. It lies within his power to do the right thing, i.e., to cultivate new powers.

Abel, a shepherd

Nothing special is said about the birth of Abel. He has no conversation with the Lord. He is connected with animal forces. In his offering he is dedicating soul-forces to the service of the divinity. He is differently constituted from his brother, with a different consciousness.

Abel is a "shepherd." The expression is symbolic. The shepherd is one who looks after his flock. Pastor is the Latin word and we use "pastoral" in the sense of caring. Caring is a priestly duty in this sense.

Cain slays his brother and is banished

With his pre-Fall consciousness Cain has no understanding of good or evil. The Lord tells him that he must learn self-control but for the moment he does not realise what is meant. Anger clouds his mind and in that state he kills Abel. He does it without compunction and when challenged by the Lord, he rejects responsibility.

Now Cain is made aware that what he has done is a crime. He must expiate it. The time of self-responsibility has come. He must develop earthly consciousness— "the ground henceforth shall not yield thee her strength." Being a fugitive and a vagabond means to seek experience of the world and of the inner self.

The Lord puts a mark on Cain

The mark is to show that Cain must not be slain but must have the opportunity of making retribution. It is a symbolic picture to show that the powers of a previous age must be metamorphosed to serve the new. Cain's powers are those of the future.

Enoch

Enoch, the name of Cain's son and the city named after him, means 'initiate.' In future there will be schools of initiation (mystery centres). Art, craftsmanship, the re-forming of the material world, will be guided by initiates from the mystery centres. The spiritual world will be re-attained via the physical by conscious effort. This is Cain's legacy.

NOAH AND THE FLOOD

Many people, and also giants, now lived on the earth but humanity had become wicked and God decided to destroy it. The Lord regretted having made humans and resolved that they, together with all living things, must be destroyed. There was, however, one just person, Noah. God spoke to him and told him of a flood to come and gave him instructions to build an ark and stock it. When the ark was completed, Noah made his dwelling there, together with his relatives and pairs of all the animals. Then it rained for forty days and forty nights and the earth was flooded. After a while God sent a wind to dry the earth. Noah sent out a raven and a dove to search for dry land and the dove brought back a leaf. Eventually the ark struck dry land and God told Noah to go forth. Noah built an altar to the Lord who promised that such a flood would not be repeated. A rainbow appeared in the sky and God said that this was a sign of the covenant—the earth would not be flooded again. Noah became a farmer, planted a vineyard and got drunk. Ham saw his father naked without feeling embarrassed. He told his brothers who then carefully covered him. Noah's descendants spread and peopled the earth.

NOTES

The story refers to the sinking of the continent of Atlantis to which reference is made in many mythologies. Noah, or Manu, as he is known elsewhere, was the leader of the sun-oracle in Atlantis, in the neighbourhood of the present Ireland. He was the most advanced leader and he was obviously still in touch with the creators of the earth, the Elohim or Spirits of Form.

The earth was not yet firm and conditions were changing in different parts. World evolution demanded a change from the spiritually-perceiving to the thinking human being. A development was taking place in human faculties, from instincts in Lemuria, to memory in Atlantis, to thinking in Post-Atlantis. Noah gathered together people sufficiently mature and, knowing that the catastrophe was coming, emigrated to the centre of Asia where conditions in the surface of the earth were consolidating. Here he set up a cultural or mystery centre from which the early Post-Atlantean civilisations were inspired.

Noah means 'peace-bringer.' Legends say that he called the place where he settled Manoah, 'the place of peace.' Legends also relate how Noah was instructed in medicine by the Archangel Raphael and wrote what he learned in a book. He learned Mathematics and Astronomy from the Adam Book of Wisdom which he had inherited.

Men had become wicked and God decided that the earth must be destroyed

In Atlantis misuse was made of spiritual powers. The atmosphere was thick and evil forces affected the elements. The mist dissolved, resulting in the flood.

Giants

At that time bodies were flexible. The physical appearance was conditioned by the soul.

Noah, a just man who walked with God

Noah was a high initiate, still in contact with the earth's creators.

Instructions for building and stocking the ark

These came directly from the Elohim. As far as Noah is concerned, the fact of having to count and measure shows the use of the intellect. The building of the ark and its journey can be taken imaginatively as a picture of an emigration, but being shut up in the ark could also signify an initiation.

The Lord tells Noah to embark

Jehovah's task is to continue the work of the Elohim.

Noah sends out the raven and the dove

In occult development, the raven is a stage of achievement, an occult messenger. The dove is an overshadowing spiritual power. In its simplest terms, the story demonstrates logical thinking.

The ark lands and Noah builds an altar

Earth conditions have changed. The Elohim tell Noah to go forth with the animals and replenish the earth. Jehovah, connected with humans and their activities, speaks of seed-time and harvest; i.e., there will be regular seasons.

A rainbow appears

The Elohim say there will be no more flooding of the earth. The mists of Atlantis have now dissolved so that another flood on this scale is not physically possible. With the disappearing mist the sun breaks through. Reaction of water and light produce the rainbow, a sign of the covenant which the Elohim make with Noah.

Noah becomes a farmer

Humans are directed towards the earth. Agriculture begins. The earth's relationship to the sun has changed and the earth will now support vegetation.

Noah plants a vine and gets drunk

The vine is an extraordinary plant. It has exuberant forces. The fruit undergoes a strong, peaceful ripening process and is extravagant in relation to the rest of the plant. It lends itself especially to wine-making. The use of alcohol in these ancient times strengthened the ego feeling, justifiable then but no longer appropriate.

Ham looks at his naked father

Ham behaves in an unseemly and disrespectful way towards his father and receives his curse. The fact of being disrespectful may indicate that Ham does not recognise the advent of a new era.

Noah's descendants spread and people the earth

Noah had three sons, Shem (Sem), Ham and Japheth. Three races are named after them. Shem or Sem means 'the name' and implies an ego quality. The Jews are Semites. Ham means 'the dark one' and the Egyptians and Canaanites, with whom the Israelites had to contend, trace their descent to him. Japheth means 'the beautiful.' The Greek and Nordic peoples are the Japhethites, bearing new spiritual impulses.

THE TOWER OF BABEL

At that time there was only one language in all the earth. Certain people journeyed from the east and came to the Plain of Shinar where they decided to stay, to make bricks and to build a city, and a tower whose top would reach to heaven. They wanted to make a name for themselves. But the Lord came down to see the city and the tower and the people were restrained and scattered. The place was named Babel because the Lord confounded the language there and scattered the people.

NOTES

At that time there was a universal language. The earth was now sufficiently solid to support buildings. Spiritual vision had been lost and the idea was evolving that the spiritual world could be reached by physical means. Different languages came into being.

One language and one speech

People understood one another through the sound element of language. Sound was the universal element. The sounds represented by *B, F,* etc. have a significance in themselves, whatever the language. According to Rudolf Steiner, sound and content were very closely allied in the old Sumerian language. With the hardening of the ground came also a hardening of the soul and the inability to penetrate into the sound element.

They came from the east

This was a group or a tribe that came from central Asia where Noah had landed.

The Plain of Shinar

The area later became Sumeria, the southern part of Babylonia.

Making bricks, building a city and a tower

These are earthly activities. Contact with the spiritual world is lost.

To make them a name

To develop ego-consciousness, an awareness of individuality.

The Lord came down and scattered them

Diversification means a variety of experience. In the variety of experience the ego awakens. The Lord is Jehovah.

Babel

There are two possible meanings. One is 'The Gate of God;' the other, 'confusion.'

Founders of the Israelite Nation

The Patriarchs: Abraham, Isaac, Jacob

ABRAHAM

Many characters of the Old Testament are not really individualities but whole generations collected together under one name. With Abraham there is a distinct personality.

Originally this great leader was not known as Abraham but as Abram. He was a descendant of Shem and to learn about his birth and boyhood we have to refer to legends.

Terah, his father, was chief commander at the court of King Nimrod in the land of Shinar. When a new star appeared in the heavens, the astrologers interpreted this as a sign of the birth of someone who would overthrow kings. This was told to Nimrod who ordered all new-born children to be slain and even pregnant mothers to be gathered together so that none would escape. Terah succeeded in hiding his wife and his son in a cave for ten years. Then the boy was sent to stay with Noah and remained with him for thirty-nine years. When he returned, he opposed Babylonian idolatry. In a legendary trial by Nimrod, he asserted his belief in the one God, i.e. the one spiritual power behind all phenomena.

In the Bible Story we are told that Abram and his family had lived in Ur of the Chaldees, a city situated in the lower portion of the Tigris/Euphrates valley, in Sumeria, which formed the southern part of Babylonia. The family had moved to Haran in the north. It was there that the Lord spoke to Abram, telling him that he had to leave and would be guided to another country and that he would become the father of a great nation.

Abram left with his wife and family, taking with him his nephew, Lot, and Lot's family. They were all herdsmen. They came into Canaan, but because of famine there, journeyed on into Egypt. After a sojourn in Egypt, Abram left, receiving gifts from the Pharaoh. We are told that he was very rich in cattle, silver and gold. Lot had flocks, herds and tents. On returning to Canaan they did not find enough pasture in one place for both families and Abram suggested that they should part company, giving Lot the choice of direction. Lot chose the fertile area in the valley of the Jordan, the area of Sodom and Gomorrah. Abram went to live in the Plain of Mamre, in Hebron. There he built an altar to the Lord and there, eventually, he was buried.

The people of Sodom were attacked by neighbouring tribes and taken captive, Lot included. He was rescued by his uncle. On his return from the campaign, Abram met Melchizedek, called King of Salem, who brought forth bread and wine and gave Abram his blessing. Abram had a vision wherein the Lord gave him all the land between the Nile and the Euphrates.

Sarai, Abram's wife, had no children and suggested that he have a child by her Egyptian maid, Hagar. The result of this union was Ishmael.

The Lord again appeared to Abram, exhorting him to be perfect. God told him that henceforth his name should be Abraham, meaning the father of many nations. The covenant was the rite of circumcision. His wife should henceforth be called Sarah and she would be a mother of nations. A child would be born to her in her old age.

One hot day Abraham had three visitors to whom he offered hospitality. After some conversation the foremost of them said that he would return in a year's time, after Sarah would have had her son. Abraham discussed with him the state of affairs in Sodom and Gomorrah and learnt from him that these cities were about to be destroyed on account of their wickedness. Abraham asked if the city would be saved if only fifty just men were found there, even forty, thirty, twenty, ten. He was assured that if only ten just men were found, the city would not be destroyed.

Lot, in the meantime, was living in Sodom. One evening, sitting at the city gate, he saw two angels approaching and he invited them into his house. The neighbours and people of the city were very curious about these visitors and demanded to know more about them. Lot went out of his house to remonstrate with the menacing crowd but the angels pulled him back again and afflicted the aggressors with blindness.

In the morning the angels advised Lot to leave the city quickly because it was about to be destroyed. He was told to take his family and not to look back. With his wife and two daughters he hurried out of the city upon which a rain of fire and brimstone began to fall. His wife looked back and was turned into a pillar of salt.

Abraham's son was born in due course and he was called Isaac (he who laughs). God challenged Abraham to offer his son as a sacrifice. Abraham took the youth, with servants, to the appointed place and prepared an altar. He put wood on it, bound lsaac and was about to make the sacrifice when the angel of the Lord called upon him to desist. He saw a ram in a thicket, took that and sacrificed it in place of the boy. Then the voice of the angel proclaimed that as he had been found obedient and worthy, he would be blessed and his descendants would be as multitudinous as the stars in heaven and the sand on the seashore.

NOTES

We have to consider conditions in the earth structure about the year 3000 B.C. In the areas with which we are concerned there were still eruptions, floods and disturbances in the earth's surface. Physical and spiritual developments are connected with one another. As earthly conditions settled, a new race, or rather a new consciousness developed. It was a corrsciousness of the material world which first came to expression in the Egypto-Chaldean epoch. This period coincides with the beginning of Kali Yuga, the dark age. The light of the supersensible was disappearing and humanity had to come to terms with the physical world.

About the year 2000 B.C. Abram, or Abraham, received his call. He was a former inhabitant of Ur of the Chaldees in Sumeria, a centre of high culture. During the period under consideration there took place a great mixing of peoples. Sumerian culture disappeared. Politically, Babylon and Egypt became powerful but spiritual awareness declined.

Abram's birth and boyhood

The legends clearly indicate a special personality. The parallel with the birth of Jesus is evident. The cave experience could be taken as a picture of inner development, of forces turning inward to bring about the change from spiritual perception to thinking. It heralds the dawn of a new consciousness. Abram's stay with Noah, real or symbolic, can be thought of as a training. When, in his trial before Nimrod, Abram asserts his own belief, he is expressing the force of his own ego.

The story could also be taken as symbolic of the struggle between old, degenerate forces and the new. The new force entering humankind is the capacity, centred physically in the brain, to develop an intellectual understanding of the world.

Ur of the Chaldees

This was a centre of culture where there was a split into esoteric and exoteric streams. The former was cherished by the Chaldees, the sages of the time; the latter came to expression in huge buildings such as pyramids and palaces.

Abram goes to a foreign land

The physical environment is an essential ingredient for a new development. By contrast with Egypt and Babylonia, Canaan was a raw land, with mountains, caves and a few fertile areas. It had not been modified by humans.

Abram has flocks and herds

He was a shepherd, a pastor, i.e., a priest/king figure.

Father of a great nation

This signifies a new consciousness, a new impulse in human development.

Haran

A mystery centre, a place of cultural/religious significance.

Abram travels to Egypt

Abram must also absorb Egyptian wisdom. Gifts from the Pharaoh signify knowledge. To his Babylonian wisdom he has now added that of Egypt.

Returning to Canaan, Abram parts company with Lot

The parting is not only a question of pasture but of world outlook. Lot was still influenced by the Babylonian inheritance and therefore chose Sodom. Nevertheless, he did not mix with the inhabitants and legends describe him as some sort of a reformer. At that time the Jordan valley must have been fertile and the Sodomites rich. Possibly Lot found it similar to his former home.

Abram meets Melchizedek

Melchizedek was called King of Salem, a priest of the most high God. *Salem* means 'peace.' He is a mysterious figure who brings bread and wine. This is in contrast to the old blood sacrifice which stimulated the old type of clairvoyance. It is a foreshadowing of the coming of Christ. According to Rudolf Steiner, Melchizedek is the reincarnated Noah, a representative of the Sun Mystery (Sun oracle of Atlantis), the same Manu who inaugurated the Indian, Persian and Egypto-Chaldean post-Atlantean cultures. Abram receives confirmation of his mission. He has to prepare the way for the Sun-Spirit who will one day become man, i.e., Jesus Christ.

Abram becomes Abraham; Sarai becomes Sarah

Abraham means 'the father of many nations' and Sarah, in modern terms, the First Lady.

Circumcision

It was the purpose of the Jewish race to provide a suitable physical vehicle for the incarnation of the Christ—hence the strict laws about behaviour and intermarriage. In a land where water is scarce there is a problem of cleanliness. Circumcision was both a matter of hygiene and a way of bringing the physical side of reproduction to greater consciousness.

The degenerate cults of the Israelites' neighbours wanted to retain the world of visionary seeing and ecstatic intoxication. The sex urge and the power of reproduction became objects of religious cult, eventually the so-called Phallus cult.

There is, however, a deeper side to the sex urge, namely, that it prepares the way for a human being to descend from the spiritual world. Copulation is therefore a spiritual act as well as a physical one. The Israelites above all, considering their mission to prepare for the incarnation of the Christ, had to be conscious of this. Circumcision was a ritual designed to emphasise the high purpose of sex.

The three visitors

In the midday heat the soul is transported to another plane. Abraham experiences the presence of Jehovah and two angels. It is an assurance of divine protection and confirmation that a son will be born in due course in spite of the age of the parents. Abraham argues a case with Jehovah for sparing the cities of Sodom and Gomorrah.

Lot lived in Sodom

This region was still subject to earthquakes and volcanic activity. The territory around Sodom, which was once fertile, is now the desert of Judea and contains the Dead Sea.

Lot had not been able to free himself entirely from the old traditions. Sodom was degenerate. The fact that he was sitting at the gate might indicate that he was at least looking outward and had distanced himself somewhat from the affairs of the city.

Angels approach

Lot, too, is under divine protection. The threat to his home and rescue is a picture of good and evil forces struggling for his soul.

Lot's wife is turned to a pillar of salt

This is a symbolic picture of not being able to renounce the old and the past. As a result the soul becomes hardened and sclerotic.

The birth of Isaac and the demand for his sacrifice

It is difficult to think of the story of the sacrifice as factual. It is symbolic.

Isaac's birth was a miracle. Abraham was 100 years old, Sarah 90. Abraham received the demand to sacrifice the boy. We might ask what then is the purpose of all the trouble bringing him into the world if he is to leave it again so quickly. Two matters are involved, one concerns Abraham; the other, Isaac. Sacrifice is an affirmation that everything belongs to God. Abraham must be willing to yield his nearest and dearest. He is being tested. It is as if God had to make sure of him.

Legends give the clue to Isaac's experience. As the knife was raised, his soul fled, returning when the angel spoke. For Isaac this was an initiation process.

The ram in the thicket

In the Platonic year the earth comes under the influence of a particular sign of the zodiac every 2160 years. This period marks the duration of a cultural epoch. The Chaldo-Egyptian epoch unfolded under the influence of Taurus, the bull. The new age of Aries, the ram, began in 747 B.C. and lasted until 1413 A.D. It was during this period that the Christ event took place.

Abraham saw the ram, i.e., he looked forward to the new age; but the ram's horns were caught in a thicket. Horns are symbols for two centres in the head connected with clairvoyance. When the ram is sacrificed, it means that in the new era people will no longer have the faculty of clairvoyance. Other abilities will develop: intellectual thinking, mathematical logic, the uses of weights and measures. Abraham is a forerunner in this development.

ISAAC

Abraham was growing old and wanted to see his son married. He sent a servant to find a wife for him from among his own people, telling him that an angel would guide him. The servant came to the appointed city and stopped to water his camels. He said to himself: "If I see a maiden with a water pitcher who gives me a drink and offers water to my camels, she will be a fit wife for Isaac." A girl came and acted exactly in accordance with what was in the servant's mind. He asked for her name and the names of her parents and was delighted to learn that he had addressed himself to relatives of his master. He asked if there might be a lodging for him at their house.

He was made welcome there and was offered hospitality. He, however, would not eat before he had explained his mission. The girl's father, brother and the girl herself were pleased with his proposition and in agreement. In due course, the chosen bride, Rebekah, set out with her servants and the guide for her new home.

Isaac was coming from the well of Lahai-roi to meditate in the field when he saw a train of camels in the distance. As they approached, he recognised his father's servant and saw his bride-to-be. Rebekah and Isaac loved one another on first sight. They were married and lived happily together but many years went by before they had children. Then the twins, Esau and Jacob, were born to them.

There was a famine in the land and the Lord told Isaac to go abroad, at the same time assuring him of the divine blessing and his future role. Isaac became rich in the foreign country. There were wells in this land which Abraham had caused to be dug but which had been stopped up by the Philistines. These Isaac opened up. People were jealous of his success and he moved to another district. Here too he caused wells to be dug. There was quarrelling over the ownership so he dug more that all might be satisfied. Then he went to Beer-sheba, built an altar and dug a well (*beer*) which he called Shebah (meaning 'oath')—hence the name of the town. He moved to Hebron where he died and was buried.

NOTES

Isaac is not dealt with very extensively in the Bible. What is very noticeable is his connection with water and with wells. His bride was found by a well and she dispenses water. Isaac lived by a well and was instrumental in digging wells. The thought of the water of life comes to mind, i.e., Isaac provided spiritual nourishment. Lahai-roi means 'the well of the living and seeing.' Water is the medium through which life can exist. Even the desert may bloom if water is available.

The servant is sent to find a wife

Abraham started the line of genealogy which leads to Christ. His son, Ishmael, by the Egyptian maid, obviously did not possess the right qualities. (His descendants embraced Islam.) It was essential to find the right wife for Isaac.

Rebekah at the well

She gives water to the servant and also to the camels. This can also be understood symbolically.

There is general agreement on the marriage

It seems as if all is pre-ordained. It is a matter of destiny.

Famine in the land

Symbolically interpreted, there is a lack of spiritual knowledge.

Isaac becomes rich with flocks and herds

He gains spiritual understanding and becomes rich within.

Digging wells

The parched soul may be revived through the water of life. Through Isaac flows some rejuvenating power, foreshadowing a greater power to come.

JACOB

When Rebekah was carrying the twins, she felt them struggling in the womb. She asked the Lord for the significance of this.

He told her that she was bearing two nations, two manner of people, one stronger than the other and that the elder should serve the younger. When they were born, Esau appeared first and Jacob had hold of Esau's heel.

Esau was rough and hairy and became a hunter while Jacob was a plain man living in his tent. Isaac loved Esau and enjoyed eating the venison which he brought but Rebekah favoured Jacob.

One day Jacob was cooking pottage when Esau came to him feeling faint and asking for food. Jacob agreed to give him some in exchange for his birthright.

Isaac was now getting old and his eyesight was failing. He called Esau to him in order to tell him of his right as firstborn, but first Isaac sent him away to get venison.

Rebekah heard what had been said and called Jacob. She advised him to disguise himself as Esau and to go to his father to get the birthright. Jacob did this while Esau was away.

Esau came back soon afterwards but Isaac told him he could not undo what was done and that now Esau would have to serve his brother. Esau became very angry and Rebekah advised Jacob to leave home. Isaac suggested that while he was away, he should also find himself a wife.

Jacob set off to stay with his uncle Laban, Rebekah's brother, and a relative of Abraham. On the way he had to rest and during the night he had a vision. He saw a ladder reaching up to heaven and angels ascending and descending upon it.

Nearing Laban's home, Jacob stopped at a well and made enquiries there of some shepherds about his uncle. They told him that his uncle was in good health and pointed out that his daughter, Rachel, was just approaching. Jacob fell in love with her and agreed to serve Laban seven years for her.

On the wedding day, Leah, an elder sister, was substituted for Rachel with the excuse that, according to the customs of the country, the younger sister could not marry before the elder. So Jacob took Leah and agreed to work another seven years to be able to marry Rachel. Both wives had sons, twelve in all, of whom Rachel was the mother of Joseph and Benjamin. Under Jacob's care the flocks increased and he himself became rich.

The time came for Jacob to leave Laban and there was a dispute over goods and cattle. This was resolved amicably although Rachel had taken some of Laban's statues unbeknownst to Jacob. Jacob sent notice to Esau of his return.

On the journey home Jacob wrestled with an angel and was victorious. From the angel, he received a new name, Israel. In the struggle his thigh was damaged.

Jacob sent gifts to Esau but Esau would not accept them. The brothers met and returned happily together to their father who died soon afterwards. Jacob gave Esau his blessing.

NOTES

This is another picture of the evolutionary process. Old and new forces struggle for mastery. Humanity is becoming independent but independence brings with it conflict. What is right at one time is not right at another and there is apparent injustice. Yet the old must give way or be transformed.

Jacob, representing the new forces, is engaged in struggle all his life. There is conflict in the womb, for the birthright (i.e., the leadership or the inheritance), over his wife, with Laban, with beings of the spiritual world. Like Odysseus in Greek mythology, Jacob has to wander from home to seek his soul, to gain wisdom.

Isaac entreats the Lord for children

Rebekah had appeared to be barren and Isaac was seventy when the twins were born. The conditions of birth are special, a sure sign of importance.

Struggle in the womb

The old and the new are always present but the new must prevail. The hold on Esau's heel is a pointer to retardation. We have the same symbolism in Achilles' heel.

Esau and Jacob are born

The name Esau means 'the hairy one.' Esau is a big man. He is a hunter and lives in the open. He belongs to the old world order but people of his type are no longer fit to lead, hence the words that the elder shall serve the younger. Rachel knew who was first in importance. Jacob likes to "sit in his tent," that is, he was better incarnated. There is a contrast here of strength versus intelligence.

Esau sells his birthright

He gives up the leading role knowing that he has no future even if he tries to keep the birthright,. Jacob is the bearer of the new impulse.

Jacob receives the birthright

It is a spiritual inheritance that descends upon him.

Jacob leaves home

Homelessness is a stage of spiritual development. Jacob is freeing himself from the old inherited faculties. At the same time he is following the call of destiny to learn and to find the right wife.

He sees angels ascending and descending

This experience shows that Jacob still has some connection with the old visionary powers. It is something that will fade with the development of the intellect. He calls the place Bethel, 'the house of God.'

He stops at the well

The event can be understood in both the real and the symbolic sense. In the latter case, here is the water of life, spiritual inspiration, possibly a mystery centre.

He stays with Laban

Laban is a kinsman of Abraham. He too is a herdsman, a pastor, a priest. Jacob stays for twenty years. For him the stay is a schooling and a training. The descriptions again are real and symbolic. He marries Leah after seven years of service to Laban, has to serve another seven for Rachel, then six for herds. The symbolism is that he has to learn by stages. He becomes rich, i.e., he gains the mystery wisdom.

Jacob leaves Laban taking goods and cattle

Laban is not too sure what secrets Jacob has learned and what he is taking with him. Hence there is a dispute. God tells Laban to make peace and recognise that Jacob has a right to them. Rachel has some of her father's images with her; i.e., she has also acquired knowledge.

He returns and meets angels

As he journeys home, the angels of God meet him; i.e., he now sees them consciously and he calls the place Mahanaim, which means 'God's hosts.'

He wrestles with an angel

Jacob overcomes the angel (Michael) and demands his blessing. Now he has power to assert himself. He receives the name Israel which means 'he who wrestled with an angel.' As the fight was over, the sun rose. It is the dawn of a new era. Jacob's thigh was damaged. The thigh fits into the hip and the hip belongs to the zodiacal sign of the Scales. Scales indicate balance. When people are supported by the cosmos they are in balance. When they become independent, they have to provide the balance for themselves.

Esau and Jacob are reconciled

Esau does not wish to accept Jacob's gifts, that is, he realises that he does not have the new capacities. However, he receives Jacob's blessing, signifying the acceptance of Jacob's supremacy.

The Story of Job

Trials, troubles and faith

At the time of the patriarchs there lived in the land of Uz a man called Job. He was a good, just, godfearing man, wealthy, with seven sons and three daughters.

One day Satan appeared before the Lord and the Lord pointed out what an exemplary person Job was. But Satan said, "True, but you have given him everything he could wish for. Let him suffer and he will curse you." So the Lord gave Satan permission to tempt Job.

Soon afterwards there came a messenger to Job who announced that all his oxen and asses had been stolen, the servants slain and he alone had escaped. While he was speaking, another messenger came to say that all Job's sheep had been destroyed and the shepherds with them; only he had escaped. As he was speaking, another servant came to announce that, as his sons and daughters were celebrating the eldest brother's birthday, the house had fallen in on them and all had perished except himself.

Job was extremely sorrowful but simply said, "The Lord giveth and the Lord taketh away. Blessed be the name of the Lord." He did not blame God.

Then Satan presented himself again before the Lord and the Lord pointed out that Job had suffered but had not lost faith. Satan answered that if Job were afflicted bodily, he would soon change and curse the Lord to his face; and the Lord gave Satan leave to subject Job to further trials.

Soon Job developed an illness such that his whole body was covered with sores and he was very sad within himself. His wife told him to curse God and die but Job answered that if one accepts the good in life, then one must also be prepared to accept the bad.

Three friends then came to visit him but seeing him in such a state, they could not speak to him for a while. Job spoke and complained of his troubles but they retorted that he must have brought them on himself through past sins or wickedness. Job protested his innocence. He declared that he had not been at fault and that he would like to know why the good sometimes suffer while the wicked apparently prosper. He said that he would like to appear before God to find what He had to say. If there is suffering, Job thinks there must be some reason for it but also some cure. He says one can find gold and silver by digging but not knowledge. There is knowledge and wisdom implanted in the world by God, but how does one find it?

Another person came to Job, Elihu. He rebuked the three for advancing their arguments and he rebuked Job for complaining, saying that one cannot always understand the ways of the Lord. Afflictions are there as teachers and the purpose of suffering is that the sufferer learns. God is not unjust.

Out of the whirlwind then came the voice of the Lord speaking to Job: "Who is it that complains about life without knowing what life is?" The Lord asks Job if he has any understanding of how the earth was created, or the stars, or how the bounds were set for the seas; whether he knew who created the sequence of night and day, rain, plants, animals. Job could think of no answers and said he would speak no more for he realised how little he understood.

Then God showed him two monsters, Behemoth and Leviathan, the former with bones of iron, the latter breathing fire. Job acknowledged that he had spoken without understanding. Now that his eyes were opened, he would be able to put the right question.

NOTES

The story is one of human development. Evil has come into the world. The Fall has taken place. There will be suffering. However, it is not suffering for wickedness but one which provides the urge for inner progress. Those on a path of spiritual development suffer trials not of their own making. It is the beginning of the way to God. Job is a figure similar to Amfortas in the Percival saga.

Humanity is no longer living in heavenly heights. Down in the physical world comes the experience of loss and sorrow. After the end of Lemuria there is a general hardening in earth conditions and in the human being. In the new physicality are the negations and trials which Job experiences. At first he cannot understand the reasons but finally he realises that they provide a path which leads to the divine.

Job's wealth

He is a spiritually-minded man, with a rich inner life.

Satan tempts him

Human beings have come into the physical world where they are subject to physical loss and suffering. With the developing ego-feeling there comes also a feeling of loneliness but at the same time a feeling of self-reliance.

His wife's and friends' advice

Their arguments represent the temptations of the lower nature. His wife suggests he deny God; his friends say God is punishing him. Job knows that there must be some good reason for his suffering and wants to learn it. He has a growing feeling of self, an awareness of his own ego.

Elihu

If wife and friends represent lower nature, then this figure is the higher, or an inner voice. Elihu explains that there is a way to acquire more knowledge.

God asks Job a few questions

Job recognises that direct knowledge has been lost. He cannot answer these questions from his normal consciousness but this realisation encourages him to seek further.

The two monsters

Job sees Ahriman and Lucifer, the two powers of evil contending for the human soul. He sees them without flinching. He has become aware of the nature of evil. He has reached the threshold of the spiritual world.

He is doubly rewarded

Now he harvests the fruits of his striving. The double wealth that Job gains is that of greater understanding and spiritual treasure.

The Israelites in Egypt

Joseph and his Brethren

JOSEPH

Joseph was a child of Jacob's old age. The father had a special affection for this child and showed it by making him a coat of many colours.

Joseph had dreams. Once he told his brothers that he had dreamt of them all binding sheaves of corn. His own had stood upright while those of his brothers had bowed towards it. The brothers were not pleased. He related another dream that sun, moon and eleven stars had bowed to him. His father rebuked him for telling these stories.

One day, while his brothers were watching their flocks, Joseph was sent by Jacob to see how they fared. The brothers saw him coming and were considering putting an end to him but Reuben persuaded them to throw him into a pit instead. Then Ishmaelites happened to come by on their way to Egypt and Joseph was retrieved from the pit and sold to them as a slave. The brothers stained his coat with animal blood and took it to Jacob who was persuaded that a wild animal had killed his favourite child. He was very grieved.

Joseph was brought to Egypt and sold to Potiphar, the captain of the guard. He proved very capable and was made governor of the household. Potiphar's wife tried to seduce him but he declined her advances. Thereupon she tore her dress and said he had attacked her. For this non-crime Joseph was put in prison. There the keeper found him so trustworthy that he put him in charge of all the other prisoners.

Two of the prison inmates had dreams which Joseph interpreted and in this way he came to the notice of Pharaoh who was having dreams which no one could explain. Pharaoh was impressed when Joseph told him that his dreams were a forecast of things to come. There would be seven years of plenty and seven years of famine. Joseph was appointed governor of Egypt and married the high priest's daughter.

Joseph took care that corn was stored during the years of plenty. When the predicted famine came, his brethren came from Canaan to buy corn. He recognised them and asked questions about their father but they did not realise to whom they were talking. When they reached home, they found their money had been returned. It was in their sacks and they were much troubled. They came again to Egypt and this time, on the way home, Joseph's cup was found in Benjamin's sack. It was put there purposely by Joseph. They returned to Egypt where Joseph made himself known to them. He told them to go home and bring his father and their families to Egypt where he would care for them. The land of Goshen was assigned to them.

NOTES

Joseph was obviously a great personality with a divine mission. He had clairvoyant faculties but developed a keen intellect, hence his administrative capacities. The state had been organised by the priesthood. Now there was a change. Joseph was not a priest. He came to Egypt about the same time as the capital was transferred from Memphis to Thebes, about 1500 B.C.

The famine may have been real but the story can also be taken as symbolic. Spiritual vision was fading. The Israelites came into a foreign land where there was a traditional culture. In foreign parts the sense of self awakens.

Joseph was the instrument whereby the Israelite race came into Egypt.

Joseph's birth and character

Joseph was the first-born of Rachel for whom Jacob had had particular affection and this was transferred to the child who was obviously very different from his brothers.

The coat of many colours

This should be translated as 'a garment of many pieces.' It was a covering similar to that which was used in cults to cover the divine image. Through colour and design it represented a summary of all the kingdoms of nature and the twelvefoldness of the cosmos. We must assume that Jacob recognised and honoured the special features and destiny of this boy.

Joseph's dreams

These are an echo of clairvoyant powers. Joseph has dreams foreshadowing the future but he relates these quite innocently to his brothers, not realising that what he says could have unpleasant consequences.

Joseph and his brethren in the field

The brothers were men of the world, unlike Joseph the dreamer. When they want to get rid of him, it is a picture for the destruction of the old power of clairvoyance. The experience in the pit could be the experience of sinking into oneself. Being sold as a slave is the experience of homelessness. Both are essential on the path of spiritual development. They strengthen the ego forces.

In Potiphar's house

A trial awaits Joseph which he surmounts. He is innocent but suffers.

In prison

This is another picture of being enclosed. The result is that his intellectual faculties develop to such an extent that he can now interpret dreams.

At Pharaoh's court

Up to now priests had been the leaders in every respect and they had received guidance through the Mysteries. Now a layman became administrator of the state. Joseph developed a logical power of thinking. State organisation through thinking was a new impulse.

He marries the daughter of the high priest

This symbolises also that Joseph gains knowledge of the Egyptian Mysteries.

Famine

Events may be real, symbolic, or both. There was a general loss of spiritual vision but knowledge was still to be found in Egypt. The brothers came to obtain this. When the money is returned, it is a sign that spiritual gifts cannot be purchased.

Joseph's cup

One is reminded of the grail or the cup of the Last Supper. The cup is the symbol for holding spiritual substance. Joseph gave his cup to Benjamin, the youngest of the brothers and the one most closely related. Joseph divines from this cup. Perhaps he wishes to convey some special message to his brother. It is difficult to find the significance of this episode.

The brethren are forgiven

Had Joseph not been sold into slavery, the whole course of history would have been different. This is, then, a recognition of the hand of destiny.

Joseph's bones are carried back to Canaan

If this is taken as symbolic as well as real, it means that the essence of Egyptian culture and wisdom was incorporated in the Jewish folk soul.

From Egypt to the Promised Land

Moses and his mission. Joshua, Balaam

MOSES

In the course of time there were new rulers in Egypt and Joseph was forgotten. They grew anxious about the growing number of Israelites in Egypt and made them their slaves. Pharaoh went so far as to decree that all the newborn Israelite boys should be thrown into the river.

One of the Israelite women managed to hide her child for three months; then she put him in an ark of bulrushes and concealed him in the vegetation by the river. He was found by Pharaoh's daughter who named him Moses, which means 'he who is drawn out.' She then engaged the mother (unbeknown to herself) to suckle him.

Moses grew up at the king's court. One day he went out to see how his brethren were faring and he saw a Hebrew fighting with an Egyptian. He went to the aid of the Hebrew and killed the other. Then he rebuked two fighting Hebrews who said that they knew he had killed an Egyptian. Moses decided to leave the country and went to the land of Midian.

Having arrived in that country, he was sitting by a well when the seven daughters of the priest of Midian came to draw water. They were driven away by some shepherds who were there but Moses intervened and helped them. They invited him to their father's house where he was made welcome. He took service with their father and married one of his daughters, named Zipporah.

Once while Moses was watching over his father-in-law's flocks, he came to the holy mountain, Horeb. The angel of the Lord appeared to him in a bush, in a flame of fire, but the bush was not consumed. He heard the voice of God from the bush, announcing himself as the God of his father, the God of Abraham, Isaac and Jacob. Then the Lord spoke to him saying that he had seen the affliction of the Israelites in Egypt and Moses was to be his chosen instrument to lead them out. Moses was told to speak with Pharaoh; but Moses asked, "Who am I that I should go to Pharaoh?" God told him that he would be with him. Then Moses asked what he should say to the people and was told to answer that the God of his fathers had sent him. If the people asked the name of this God, he was to say: It is the I AM. I AM has sent me, the Lord God of your fathers has sent me, the God of Abraham, Isaac and Jacob.

Moses expressed doubt as to whether the people would listen and the Lord told him to throw his rod to the ground. It became a serpent. He was then told to pick it up by the tail. It became a rod again. He was told to put his hand in his bosom. It became leprous. When taken out, it was restored. He was told to do these signs as proof that he spoke in the name of the Lord God. If the people still did not believe, he was to pour water on the land and it would turn to blood. Moses was hesitant about his ability to speak and the Lord told him that Aaron, his brother, would be appointed as spokesman.

The Lord gave further instructions. Moses and Aaron returned to Egypt to ask Pharaoh to release their people. The result was that the Egyptians increased their burden and the Israelites complained. The Lord promised to intervene.

God spoke to Moses and said, "I am the Lord. I appeared to Abraham, Isaac and Jacob as God Almighty, but by my name, JEHOVAH, I was not known to them. Say to the people, 'The Lord God of your fathers has sent me.' Go to Pharaoh, I have set thee in God's stead before Pharaoh, and Aaron, thy brother, shall be thy prophet."

Moses and Aaron came before Pharaoh. Aaron cast down his rod and it became a serpent. The wise men cast down their rods and they became serpents, but Aaron's swallowed them up.

Pharaoh would not release the Israelites and Moses and Aaron brought down on them the ten plagues. Before the last one (the slaying of the firstborn), the Lord ordered all Israelite households to smear their doorposts with the blood of a lamb. The plague would then pass over these houses.

Finally, the Israelites were allowed to leave. They were led by a pillar of cloud by day and a pillar of fire by night. Pharaoh changed his mind and sent his armies to bring them back. The Israelites reached the shore of the Red Sea. Moses was told to stretch out his hand. The waters parted and the people crossed on dry land. The Egyptians followed but at the behest of the Lord, Moses stretched forth his hand again and the waters closed over them.

The Israelites were thirsty and Moses turned bitter water into sweet. They were hungry and the Lord sent manna. They journeyed on and were thirsty again. At Horeb, Moses struck a rock and produced water. They fought the Amalekites. They met Jethro, the priest of Midian, and Moses' father-in-law. Moses received some advice from him regarding the instructions he should give to his people and the appointment of deputies.

The congregation reached Mount Sinai. On the instructions of the Lord they remained at the foot of the mountain while Moses ascended into the smoke and fire. There he received from the Lord God the Ten Commandments and stone tablets in which they were engraved. He received orders to build the Tabernacle and an ark for the Covenant. Aaron was appointed High Priest.

Moses was on the mountain for forty days and forty nights and while he was gone, the people became restless. They persuaded Aaron to make a golden calf for them to worship. When Moses returned, he was furious, destroyed it, ground it to dust, mixed the remains with water and made the people drink it. In his anger, Moses broke the tablets.

The Lord told him to get two more tablets and to come again to him on the mountain. There the Lord dictated to him the covenant, the Ten Commandments, and Moses wrote them down on the stone. When he returned from the mountain, the skin of his face shone and the people were afraid to approach him. The children of Israel continued their journey. When a cloud was over the Tabernacle, they rested, sometimes for days or weeks. When it lifted, either by day or by night, they journeyed onwards.

Again they expressed discontent and were sent a host of

quails. When they ate them, the Lord smote the people with a great plague. Miriam and her brother, Aaron, grumbled about the fact that Moses had married an Ethiopian woman but they were reprimanded by the Lord. Miriam was struck with leprosy and had to remain outside the camp for seven days, after which she was healed and allowed back.

Moses now sent twelve scouts into Canaan to reconnoitre, among them Joshua and Caleb. They came back with a report of a land flowing with milk and honey but peopled by huge men with strongly walled cities. They brought back a huge bunch of grapes, pomegranates and figs. The people rebelled at the news but Joshua quietened them.

Korah and several others, together with two hundred and fifty princes of the Israelites, began to question the authority of Moses. They were told to come to the Tabernacle and present themselves before Moses and Aaron. They came, with others of the congregation, except for Korah and two others. Moses told those of the assembly who wished to disassociate themselves from the rebels to stand clear. Then the three leaders were swallowed up by the earth and fire destroyed the two hundred and fifty. A plague broke out but it was stopped by Aaron.

To end the trouble, the Lord, through Moses, ordered all the tribal leaders to take a rod each, to put their names on them and place them in the Tabernacle. The next morning Aaron's rod had blossomed.

Again there was no water and the people murmured. Moses now doubted his ability to produce it but struck a rock nevertheless. Only at the second stroke did water flow.

Other difficulties gave rise to discontent but fiery serpents appeared, biting people. Moses made a serpent of brass and put it on a pole. Whoever looked at it was cured of his wound.

The children of Israel were now near the promised land. Aaron died and was buried on Mount Hor. Moses was a very old man. God had told him that he would not enter the new country but he would be allowed to see it. Moses appointed Joshua to succeed him and climbed to the top of Mount Nebo from where he could view Canaan. He reminded the Israelites of their god and his laws, blessed them and died. To this day noone knows where his grave is.

NOTES

The exodus from Egypt is contemporary with the fall of Troy. The ancient world of divinely led humanity gives way to that of individual, independent personalities with ego characteristics. The Israelites are experiencing homelessness. Homelessness is a step on the path of spiritual development. The old mysteries required a sinking of consciousness. In the future a heightened consciousness is demanded. It comes through the power of thought.

In 1479 B.C. the battle of Megiddo took place and the Egyptian, Thutmose III, became ruler of a great empire which included Palestine, Syria, Babylonia and Assyria. It was a worldly empire. As the spiritual world receded, the physical became important.

During the period of this empire Moses was born. This was about the year 1330 B.C. at a time when the story of the death of Osiris originated in Egypt.

Between 1304 and 1237 B.C. Ramses II, the Great, ruled in Egypt and built tremendous temples, towns and statues, using the Israelites as slaves. The exodus took place during his reign, about 1290 B.C.

The Israelites spent forty years in the wilderness. Forty years were not required to cover the distance concerned. It might have been done in forty days but sufficient time had to elapse for the Egyptian generation to die out. Moreover, the survivors had to experience the realities of the harsh physical world. Earth forces were still active. Their god was drawing near to the earth and he was experienced in the earthly elements. Moses experienced him in fire, smoke and lightning. The prophets, at a later stage, experienced him within.

In his lectures, *Christ and the Human Soul,* Rudolf Steiner speaks of these events. Between the creator gods (the Elohim),

Jehovah and Christ there is a close connection. Christ is a manifestation of the Elohim; Jehovah is his servant. Christ was worshipped by many different peoples under a different name as a being of the sun-sphere. He descended to the earth in stages before incarnating in the body of Jesus. During the Moses era the Christ being was in the earth's atmosphere; hence the Jews experienced him in the elements— as a pillar of cloud and a pillar of fire.

There is dispute among scholars as to the actual location of Mount Sinai, as well as of the actual route taken by the Israelites. This is not helped by the fact that the Bible gives two different names for the place where Moses received the tablets, Sinai and Horeb.

It is probable that the Israelites spent many years in an area which lies between the northern end of the Gulf of Aqaba and the Dead Sea, where there are oases. Nearby were Hor Mountain and Petra, a holy place. The mountains designated Sinai and Horeb were probably two mountains in the neighbourhood or two peaks of the same mountain.

Massacre of the children

Mother and child are surrounded by spiritual substance. When children are slain, forces are released which can be used in black magic. The normally prepared destiny is thwarted. Think of the historical consequences if Moses had been killed.

Moses in the ark of bulrushes

This is an imaginative picture. The child was protected. The historical probability is that there were circles in Egypt who were aware of events. They recognised this child and his mission. The palace was nowhere near the Nile. Being adopted by Pharaoh's daughter means that Moses learned Egyptian wisdom.

Moses slays an Egyptian

The significance of this story is that Moses overcame the Egyptian decadence within himself. He had spent forty years in

Egypt. Now he went to the priest of Midian, Jethro, and stayed for forty years. He acquired another type of learning.

Sitting by the well

The well is not necessarily one which yields water. It indicates a spiritual atmosphere. It dispenses the water of life. The seven daughters of Midian represent an experience of soul forces. When Moses fought off the aggressive shepherds, he was withstanding a trial. Marrying one of the daughters means that he was accepted into the holy circle. The place was probably a mystery centre. The fact that he married Zipporah, 'the dark one,' is symbolic of the shadow world of the intellect.

The experience on Horeb

The divinity spoke to Moses through the elemental forces of fire and smoke. The fire that Moses saw was a spiritual experience, hence the reason why the bush did not burn. He saw the Archangel Michael, then experienced the Christ without recognising Him in his true nature.

The experience of the presence of the Elohim was too great for the moment and Moses hid his face. His consciousness contracted to the awareness of Jehovah who told him that his mission was to lead the Israelites out of Egypt.

The name of the divinity

Moses asked the Elohim to confirm his mission and asked further what he must say when the people wanted to know who had sent him, and, in particular, wanted a name. The Elohim answer: "Say I AM has sent you. Say, Jehovah Elohim has sent you. Say, the Elohim have sent you."

Asking after the name means asking after the nature and the nature of the Elohim is I AM. The significance of this conversation becomes clearer after further talk among Moses, Jehovah and the Elohim. In the meantime there is a shift of scene where Jehovah told Moses that Pharaoh must release the children of Israel.

The rod turns into a serpent

The serpent was an expression used in the old world for supersensible forces. "Serpents" was also a name for initiates. The act with the serpent is connected with a change of consciousness and also with the development of physical human being. The serpent was the fifth animal to appear with a spinal column, and when the human being acquired a spinal column, there came with it a faint feeling of ego-consciousness. Their etheric at one time stretched out above the head and below the feet into the ground and this connection gave spiritual perception. The expression "The serpent is active within me" means that the etheric stretches upwards and downwards and gives vision.

The rod is an inner experience, thinking. When the rod turns into a serpent, it is a sign that Moses has spiritual vision. When he grasps it by the tail and it becomes a rod again, it is a picture of the backbone in man which leads to the brain and points to the fact that future spiritual vision is to be acquired through thinking. Moses has the old faculty of clairvoyance but also he leads from the dreamland of ancient vision to the awakened land of thinking.

Moses complains that he is not a speaker

To help Moses, Jehovah appointed Aaron. In Egypt the priests were able to use language so that it had a hypnotic effect. It is to be assumed that Aaron was familiar with this and had the same power. There was a certain magic in his use of language.

Jehovah announces himself

The Bible says: God spoke to Moses. . . . and then the singular person is used. Taking the Elohim as the equivalent of God, it is difficult to use "I." But the Elohim are experienced as a unity; therefore one might say: the Elohim spoke to Moses collectively, saying "I appeared unto Abraham, Isaac and Jacob by the name of God Almighty but by my name Jehovah I was not known unto them."

The Elohim, having announced themselves as the I AM, now equate themselves with Jehovah. Jehovah is their name.

This seeming riddle is solved by considering the meaning of the word Jehovah. It has a dual significance. In the sounds JHVH is incorparated the meaning 'I AM' but there is also a meaning 'he who creates.' Thus the Elohim declare their nature. Elohim, Jehovah Elohim, Jehovah, are aspects of the one unity, the I AM. At the same time they are the creators. (Dr. Steiner gives the actual meaning of Jahve [Jehovah] as 'I AM the I AM.')

Christ is a manifestation of the Elohim and through His power gives man the possibility of realising himself as an "I am." Jehovah reflected the Christ light until man could receive it directly.

It was the task of Moses to lead the people from spiritual vision and group consciousness to thinking and individual ego-consciousness. His message to the people was that the time had come for the realisation of the individual, the ego. The divinity he experienced on Mount Horeb is the same as appeared later as the Christ.

Moses and Aaron before Pharaoh: The contest

The old forces were not yet entirely discarded. The rod could become a serpent and the serpent, a rod. When Moses and Aaron threw down their rods, they were moving in the sphere of clairvoyance. The priests of Pharaoh did likewise but Aaron's rod swallowed the others, i.e., he was the more powerful. He predicted the future.

The plagues

The ten plagues were a spiritual experience brought about for the Egyptians by Aaron's magic power of the word. They were not real in the physical sense. The events were not only produced to ensure the release of the Israelites but they were a prophetic demonstration of the future of Egypt. The plagues were: 1) Water turns to blood. 2) Frogs. 3) Lice. 4) Flies. 5) Cattle disease. 6) Boils and sores. 7) Hail and fire from heaven. 8) Locusts. 9) Darkness. 10) Death of the firstborn.

A change was taking place in the physical/spiritual constitution of human beings. The etheric body which had extended beyond the physical in both directions was contracting into the physical. With the loss of spititual vision the soul felt confined. Thus the water into blood signifies a closer connection of the etheric with the physical. The plagues 2–8 were a sort of itch caused by the changing nature of the etheric and astral bodies. The darkness (9) is the loss of spiritual vision. The death of the firstborn (10) is a picture of the ego leaving the spiritual world and entering the physical.

The death of the firstborn did not apply to the Israelites because they were already developing ego-consciousness in the physical. This is the significance of smearing their door with lamb's (ram's) blood, the Passover. As the human being's etheric contracted and natural clairvoyance faded, a certain projection was still felt above the head and this became the picture of the ram with its horns. When the ram is sacrificed (cf. Abraham), it signifies that thinking is supplanting vision. The great change was one of consciousness.

Pillars of cloud and pillars of fire

Cloud and fire. Jehovah manifests himself in the elements.

Crossing the Red Sea

It is questionable whether in fact the Israelites did cross the Red Sea. If they did, then the explanation would be that Moses, with the dawning intellectual faculty could reckon out the movement of the tides and wind and act accordingly. Modern scholars, however, think that a crossing was made of the Sea of Reeds, a freshwater lake. It may have been shallow or swampy but Moses had the mentality to find the way across.

The Israelites are thirsty and hungry

They are thirsty and hungry in a double sense, physically and spiritually. Moses provided the water. Jehovah sent manna. Physically, manna was something that looked like coriander seed. It could be milled and ground and made into a sort of cake. It was formed by the dew reacting with certain substances in the earth. Finding this substance unexpectedly also provided an uplifting experience for the soul. It appeared to come through divine grace and it came in the night.

The word *manna* is connected with *Manas*, a higher faculty of the human being, also with *Manu* (Noah) the 'thinking' leader from Atlantis and with *man*.

When Moses struck the rock, water gushed forth. Perhaps Moses had the ability to judge where water might be found but the story is also symbolic. Moses provided inspiration.

The desert experience must have been traumatic. Desert can be equated with loneliness, emptiness, sterility. The soul is parched and thrown back on itself. There were periods of joy and periods of grief. The one strengthens the will, the other leads to understanding. Ego forces were required in order to survive.

Jethro

The Israelites were led by Moses to Jethro, his father-in-law. According to Dr. Bock (*Moses und sein Zeitalter*),. Jethro was the leader of a mystery centre at Kadesh and it was here that Moses had already spent forty years after fleeing from Egypt. Now the whole people came and were probably instructed by Jethro. Nearby was the spring which Moses caused to flow and in the neighbourhood were Mount Sinai/Horeb. The Israelites stayed here many years.

Sinai

In the thunderings and lightnings, the smoke and the fire, Moses was aware of the Elohim. From Jehovah he received his instructions concerning the building of the Tabernacle and an ark to house the Covenant. This consisted of the stone tablets on which the Ten Commandments and other directives were written.

With regard to the Ten Commandments, these are mostly negatives, giving clear guidance as to what should *not* be done. The

Israelites were not yet sufficiently mature to decide for themselves. The ego forces were not yet fully awake. The commandments have nothing to do with sin and redemption and are required to be understood through the intellect.

In building a tabernacle, Moses was to inaugurate a cult. In it were symbols of the macrocosm and the elements. There were seven sections representing the seven days of creation, twelve pieces of shewbread (loaves displayed and renewed each Sabbath), seven candles, four different coloured materials representing the four elements.

The golden calf

The Israelites had become restless during Moses' absence and resurrected the old form of worship. Taurus was the sign of the Zodiac under which the Egyptian culture had flourished. Similar stories of aberration mean embracing old beliefs.

The second visit to Sinai

Moses replaced the tablets and Jehovah dictated to him the words of the commandments. The first ones were written with the finger of God. The new ones were written by human hand, i.e., the human being takes over responsibility.

His skin shone

The physical body had become radiant through the spirit within.

Clouds over the tabernacle

In certain areas there was still volcanic activity or a movement in the earth. The journey could only be continued when conditions were suitable.

The people complain again

Quails were sent which caused illness and a plague followed. This signifies something similar to the experience of the plagues in Egypt. Soul and spirit were feeling uncomfortable in changed circumstances.

The twelve scouts

The report of a huge people means that the scouts saw clairvoyantly the projecting etheric bodies of the Canaanites, who were now in a state of decadence. The huge bunch of grapes points to Canaan as a land of primeval forces.

Korah's rebellion

Korah wanted to establish a sort of democracy before it was time. The rebels were destroyed by an earthquake or volcanic activity.

Lack of water

Moses faltered. He had to strike the rock twice. He and Aaron, great as they were, could not enter the promised land because they were still part of the old world.

The brazen serpent

The Israelites were tired of shortages and hardship and longed for the former Egyptian spiritual experiences. The volcanic area loosened their minds and awakened the old spiritual experiences but in the changed times these experiences were chaotic. This is symbolized by the fiery serpent which bit the people, i.e., brought about illness, mental or physical. The cure was the assertion of the ego.

The staff is the staff of the ego, the straight backbone. The serpent, fastened by its head to the staff, symbolises the triumph of the ego forces over the chaotic spiritual experience.

BALAAM AND HIS ASS

The Israelites had to struggle with various peoples in various stages of decadence. Balak, King of the Moabites, asked Balaam, a magician, to curse the Israelites and to help him to fight them. God warned Balaam against this in his dreams and Balak's demands were refused.

Balak repeated the request, offering great rewards but again Balaam was warned in his dreams. He went, however, to visit Balak, riding on his ass but the way was barred by an angel, which the ass saw but he did not. He beat the animal, which complained of unfair treatment. Then Balaam became aware of the angel who reprimanded him but told him to proceed and to repeat to Balak what he, the angel, had to say. This Balaam did and explained that the Israelites were under God's protection and had a messianic mission.

NOTES

The one who would curse the Israelites is converted by divine intervention and ends up blessing them. Balaam had already been warned in dreams. He set out in a doubtful frame of mind. The ass being barred by an angel, which Balaam did not see, signifies that something in his nature held him back, which he repressed. Then the presentiment which he had rejected came to consciousness; he realised the truth and the message he had to deliver.

Appointment of Judges: Gideon, Samson, Samuel

Guidance and encouragement

The twelve tribes occupied territories which suited their character. They settled down together with the original inhabitants. In the Old Testament record we now have the period of the judges. It must be understood that the term judges is not meant in any legal sense. Judges were the appointed leaders who gave directives to the people. They presided over a period when there was a great deal of opposition to be overcome. Their activity lies between the years 1200–1020 B.C.

GIDEON

One of the judges was called Gideon. He was called to serve his people at a time when they were oppressed by the Midianites. These peoples had once been in the forefront of development but now they were no longer so.

One day, Gideon was threshing wheat secretly, in an attempt to keep it from his masters, when he became aware of an angel speaking to him. Gideon was being called upon to save his people. He doubted his senses but made an offering which the angel touched with his staff and which was then immediately consumed by fire. This convinced him that his visitor was truly the Angel of the Lord.

Gideon's first task was to destroy the altar of Baal. He then asked God for a further sign that he had been chosen to lead his people. He put out a sheep's fleece, the sign of assent to be that it should become wet and the area around it dry. On a second occasion the fleece should be dry and the surroundings wet. These signs were given.

He then had to choose the right companions for the task of overcoming the enemy. The Lord told him that the numbers should be limited, otherwise the people would boast of their own power and overlook their god. From the ranks of the Israelites

Gideon told those who were afraid to step out. Twenty-two thousand took the offer. Ten thousand were left. The Lord told Gideon to take them to a brook and tell them to drink. He was to choose those who took water in their hand and then lapped it like a dog. Of these there were three hundred.

Gideon and his servant then went near the Midianite camp and overheard soldiers talking. One said that he had dreamt of a loaf of barley tumbling into their camp and overturning a tent. A second interpreted this as the sword of Gideon and an omen of their defeat.

The three hundred Israelites were divided into hundreds, given trumpets and pitchers and ordered to surround the enemy camp at night. At a given signal they blew on their trumpets and broke the pitchers. The Midianites fled.

After this there was peace in the land for the rest of Gideon's lifetime, forty years.

NOTES

Again the Israelites are seduced, subjugated, and again a leader is appointed to free them. Again it is demonstrated that spiritual power is stronger than physical. Again it is the forces of the intellect which prevail.

Gideon threshes wheat

The threshing floor is often used as a picture for a holy place. This holy place is in the soul. Gideon's experiences are spiritual.

The wet and dry fleeces

The fleece, belonging to the ram, is used as a symbol of clairvoyance. Gideon wants assurance that he has perceived correctly.

Three hundred are chosen

Strength does not lie in numbers, but in spiritual power.

Lapping the water

This is difficult to interpret. Perhaps the significance lies in the fact that a dog is intelligent and wary. Those drinking like a dog have the necessary wakefulness.

The victory

There was no battle. Outwardly victory was won by a stratagem, the use of the intellect. In another sense it was spiritual power that prevailed.

JOSHUA

On the death of Moses the Lord appointed Joshua to be the leader of the Israelites. He was told to obey the Lord's commandments and laws and he was promised support.

The children of Israel were now near the promised land and Joshua sent out two spies. They lodged in Jericho with a woman called Rahab but the king of the country was informed of the presence of spies and sent out his men to search for them. Rahab hid the two Israelites and then let them down over the city wall. They told her to put a red ribbon in her window as a sign, so that when the city was conquered, she and her family would not be harmed. When the spies returned to Joshua, they reported that the inhabitants of Jericho were feeling faint at the approach of the invaders.

There came the moment to cross the Jordan. The priests took the Ark of the Covenant and went first into the river, which stopped its flow, allowing all the people to cross on dry land. When they reached the opposite bank, the water flowed again. A circle of twelve stones was erected and the place was called Gilgal.

Joshua had a vision of an archangel who announced himself as Captain of the Lord's Hosts and who said that the place was holy ground.

The Israelites reached Jericho, a walled and fortified city. According to the Lord's instructions for capturing it, seven priests marched round it once a day for six days, bearing the Ark of the Lord and blowing on trumpets of ram's horns. The seventh day they went round seven times, then gave a blast. on the horns accompanied by shouts of the people. The walls collapsed. Orders were given that Rahab and her famiiy be spared.

There was to be no looting or wrongdoing but one Israelite took some gold and silver for himself and hid it.

The Lord was angry and in the next battle, at Ai, the Israelites were defeated as punishment for the theft. The culprit was found and put to death. Then Ai was conquered by a stratagem: the Israelites pretended to flee, drew the defendants out of their strong position, then turned and attacked. At the victory celebration Joshua wrote down a copy of the law of Moses on the altar stones.

Another race, the Gibeonites, aware of what had happened at Jericho and Ai, were afraid, and came to Joshua pretending to be poor. They dressed in old clothes, had stale bread and old wine in their packs, and asked for an alliance. Joshua agreed but then found that they were not so poor after all. He kept his promise, however, but made them servants and slaves.

There followed many struggles and battles with other peoples until much territory was acquired. On one occasion the Gibeonites were attacked by their neighbours but the Israelites defended them. On this occasion Joshua called on the sun and moon to stand still so that the Israelites could consolidate their victory.

Joshua shared out the land among the different tribes. He grew old, called the leaders of the tribes, admonished them to keep the law of Moses, reminded them that they were now in the promised land, took his farewell, and died.

NOTES

Whereas Moses was very much the instrument of the divine will, Joshua appears to have a much more human element. Moses is the promise, Joshua the fulfilment.

Joshua was known as the son of Nun. Nun is not a family name but a sort of title of honour. Actually Nun means 'fish.' A fish swims in water. Water is often used as a picture of the etheric. Thus the title is meant to convey that Joshua had some special power.

With Joshua the promised land had been reached. Now it had to be acquired.

Rahab protects the spies

Even in Jericho there were individuals who knew of coming developments. Feeling faint could refer to their own loss of spiritual sustenance or the feeling that coming events would be irresistible.

Crossing the Jordan

This is an event similar to the crossing of the Red Sea. It is not only a geographical matter but also a spiritual one—the promised land, a new sphere.

The stone circle

Gilgal means 'wheel of the sun.' Christ, the spirit of the sun, was approaching.

The destruction of Jericho

It is difficult to be specific as to events. Sound can have a shattering effect but that city walls should fall down as a result of a few trumpets being blown and people shouting is a little hard to believe; however, the event is not hard to understand symbolically.

Jericho was situated in a remnant of fertile ground which had all around been destroyed by volcanic activity. Perhaps there was an earthquake. No actual attack is recorded. The city was decadent. The spiritual force of the Israelites may have won the day as did the pope when confronted by Attila.

One Israelite took gold and silver

He was seduced by old beliefs and practices. The transgression brought retribution at Ai.

Struggles with local tribes

These were undoubtedly physical and spiritual. The Canaanites possessed old powers of spiritual vision which they were reluctant to give up. Ai was overcome by a stratagem. This shows the use of the intellect.

When the Gibeonites brought stale bread and old wine, they were demonstrating that they recognised that their spiritual resources were outmoded. They were poor in spirit although they had certain traditions. To ask for an alliance means that they wished to join the new impulse.

When the Gibeonites were attacked, Joshua supposedly cried for the sun and moon to stand still. As recorded in our Bible this is a wrong translation. The call was a supplication to the spiritual being of the sun: "Spirit of the Sun, shine on Gibeon." It inspired confidence in the Israelite armies.

Joshua copies the law of Moses onto stone

This is a reaffirmation in the new territory. It is a confirmation that the outer world must be conquered by the inner. In that Joshua did the work, it stresses the human element.

SAMSON

Samson was another *judge* of the Israelites. At the beginning of this story their wrongdoing had brought about their subjugation to the Philistines.

A man called Manoah had a wife who so far had borne no children. One day there came an angel to her announcing that she would bear a son. She was told not to drink wine or to eat anything unclean. The boy must not have his hair cut; he must be brought up a Nazarite. The angel promised that this child would begin to deliver the children of Israel out of the hands of their oppressors and that the Lord would guide him.

The boy was born in due course and was called Samson. He grew up to be a very strong man. Having attained manhood, he fell in love with a Philistine woman, to the disgust of his parents. Once on the way to visit her he slew a lion and on his return he found a swarm of bees and honey in the carcass. He took some of the honey and brought it to his parents.

He married the woman and thirty men of her race attended the wedding. He asked them a riddle, to be solved within seven days, promising thirty sheets and thirty changes of garment to the guests for the answer, but stipulating the equivalent to himself if no solution were forthcoming. The riddle was:

> Out of the eater came forth meat (food or nourishment)
> And out of the strong came forth sweetness.

The Philistines were perplexed and asked Samson's wife to find the answer, threatening to burn down her father's house if she did not obtain it. She pleaded with Samson, received it, and gave it to the guests:

> What is sweeter than honey:
> and what is stronger than a lion?

Samson realised that his wife had given away the secret. He went to Ashkelon, killed thirty men and took their garments to make the payment. He was cross, went back home but found his father-in-law had given his wife to someone else, saying that he thought Samson hated her. The younger sister was offered in her place. Samson was angry. He caught three hundred foxes, tied torches to their tails and drove them through the Philistines' crops. As a result the house of his father-in-law was set on fire and father-in-law and wife died. Samson went away.

The Philistines went to the men of Judah and asked them to capture Samson. Samson agreed to be tied up but then he broke loose and killed a thousand men with the jawbone of an ass. He was thirsty and the Lord made water come from the jawbone.

One day Samson went to Gaza. The Philistines thought that this would be a good opportunity to catch him. They lay in wait, intending to seize him first thing in the morning when he appeared. Samson got up at midnight, took the doors of the city gate, together with the two posts, bar and all, and carried them to the top of a hill near Hebron.

He fell in love with a woman called Delilah. The Philistines asked her to find out the secret of his strength. He teased her. He said that he should be bound with seven green withies. Then he broke loose. He suggested that he should be bound with new ropes. These he burst. The third proposal was to weave the seven locks of his hair with the web of the loom. He freed himself. Finally he confessed that if his hair were cut, he would lose his strength. Delilah was bribed. She arranged for his hair to be cut off while he was asleep. His strength was gone and he was taken captive. He was put in prison and blinded. His hair began to grow again. One day the Philistines fetched him out of prison to make fun of him. He was put in front of the temple which was crowded with people, even on the roof. He felt for the pillars, pushed two down and died with thousands of others.

NOTES

Samson certainly provides us with some strange stories which the most credulous could scarcely believe literally. Although called upon to free his people, he seems to have spent his time annoying the enemy although finally he did destroy their temple. Most of the story has to be understood symbolically. Divine powers are represented as physical strength.

Samson's birth and upbringing

All the ingredients are present to show that we are concerned with a special personality. The mother was apparently barren; the angel came and predicted a birth. The angel gave instructions about his upbringing and his mission.

Nazarite

The Nazarites were a sect abstaining from alcohol, vinegar and animal products. They were vegetarians in the strictest sense and grew their hair long. Long hair denotes a special connection with spiritual forces. When the hair is cut, the etheric forces are compressed into the physical. In those days it meant a loss of spiritual vision which the Nazarites wished to retain. Eating animal foods also mitigated against spiritual vision. The Korah people present a contrast. They were thinkers. Korah means 'bald.'

At the same time spiritual vision was fading and thinking was developing. It was a period of transition. Samson had both faculties.

Samson takes a Philistine wife

The significance of this is that Samson takes an interest in Philistine culture and religious observances.

Slaying the lion

The picture indicates that Samson had mastered his animal nature, at least at that point. Overcoming this leads to the spirit, i.e., bees and honey. He takes some inspiration to his parents.

The wedding feast

He unites with Philistine culture but is not entirely at home. He tests their beliefs with a riddle. The answer itself is no real answer but almost another riddle.

"That which is sweeter than honey and stronger than a lion." The inference is that it is spirit or spiritual knowledge.

The foxes

The fox is an animal of great cunning. If Samson could catch three hundred foxes, he must have had exceptional powers, not only of physical strength. The episode points to powers of intellect. The torches on the tails are perhaps a picture of Samson's inner strength. The Philistines are disconcerted; i.e., their way of life is questioned.

Samson is bound but breaks loose

Earthly ties cannot bind the spirit. Samson's strength is spiritual.

The jawbone of an ass

The picture this object is intended to convey is problematical. The ass is closely related to the horse. Horses were not so common. The horse is a symbol for the enlightened intellect. Perhaps this is another example of thought gaining the mastery over instincts.

The gate of Gaza transported to Hebron

The new path to knowledge was inaugurated by Abraham who was buried in Hebron. Transplanting the gate means crossing the threshold in a new way.

Delilah

Samson was still engrossed with Philistine culture yet confident of his own superior powers. He was bound but freed himself. Again it is a picture of higher spiritual powers overcoming the physical. The Philistines want his secret. He was blinded and his hair cut off, i.e., he was deprived of spiritual vision but his faculties return and he destroys the temple, i.e., the old rites.

SAMUEL

Another of the great judges of the Israelites was Samuel. His father was a man called Elkanah and his mother, Hannah. They loved one another very much but had no children. One day, Hannah prayed to the Lord that she might have a son but as she did not speak loudly and only moved her lips, the priest, Eli, accused her of being drunk. She explained what she was doing and Eli expressed the hope that her wish would come true. She promised the Lord that if her desire were fulfilled, the boy would be dedicated to the service of the temple and would be brought up a Nazarite.

In due course a son was born and, when he was old enough, he was sent to serve the priest.

Eli, in the meantime, was becoming blind and Samuel served in the temple. One evening, when he was about to lie down to sleep, he heard a voice calling him. He thought the voice was Eli's and went to him, but Eli had not called. This happened three times, then Eli realised that it was the voice of the Lord which Samuel heard. The message was that, because of the evil which Eli's sons had done and the fact that Eli had not restrained them, his family was not fitted for leadership and Samuel must take over the responsibility.

At that time there was again war between the Israelites and the Philistines and the latter were victorious. In the hope that it would help their cause, the Israelites brought out the Ark of the Covenant although it was unlawful to do so. The Philistines captured it and put in in their temple beside the idol of their god, Dagon. In the morning the idol had fallen down. They set it up again but the next morning it was on the floor in pieces. The Philistines realised that there was some mighty power about the Ark and decided to get rid of it, but wherever it was taken, there occurred some plague or misfortune. After seven months they gave it back to the Israelites, with gifts.

In the meantime, Samuel had become judge. He encouraged and stimulated his people to great efforts until the Philistines were defeated.

Samuel travelled much about the country, giving advice and directives but when he became old, his sons were appointed. They, however, proved themselves unjust men, taking bribes and not fulfilling their duties and there came a time when the people decided they wanted a king. They declared that they wished to be like the other nations around them.

Samuel asked the Lord for advice and was told to explain what it would mean to have a king. He told the people how they would have to work harder, be subject to new burdens and pay tithes, but still they persisted.

Guided by the Lord, Samuel was led to find a certain person called Saul, whom he anointed as king. Saul, however, proved unworthy after a time and Samuel was instructed to find another. The new king was David.

NOTES

Samuel was the last of the judges. At the beginning of his story appear the words "And the word of the Lord was precious in those days." The significance of the quotation is that spiritual vision was fast fading. Samuel leads over to the kings who are more concerned with the earthly world.

Birth and upbringing

As with other great personalities, there are special circumstances.

Eli's blindness

This is possibly physical but more likely it indicates a loss of spiritual vision.

The voice of the Lord

Samuel is still in direct contact with the spiritual world. His faculty of seership enables him to find the kings.

The effect of the presence of the Ark

The new forces are more powerful than the old. The races still enveloped in old spirituality cannot cope with them.

Appointing a king

This is a turning point; Paradise, divine guidance, are left behind. A king is an earthly ruler.

The Story of Ruth

A time of harmony and fulfilment

RUTH

At one period during the time of the Judges there was famine. A certain man and his wife and two sons emigrated from Bethlehem to the east of Jordan. The sons married there but after a time all the men died and the old widow decided to return to her home. She wanted her two daughters-in-law to stay but one of them, Ruth, decided to go with her. "Thy people shall be my people and thy god, my god," she said.

They came back to Bethlehem at harvest time and Ruth gleaned in the field. Boaz, the owner, was much taken with her, told her to eat and drink with the reapers and encouraged the reapers to leave a little extra grain on purpose. Ruth did the master some service and received measures of barley as payment. Boaz was so attracted to Ruth that he finally married her. One of their descendants was David, the king.

NOTES

Bethlehem was a green oasis-like area in the middle of desert, like Hebron to the south, and Galilee and Damascus to the north. Bethlehem means 'the house of bread' and according to Dr. Steiner, it was an ancient mystery centre of the Adonis cult. Rachel, Jacob's wife, died there, giving birth to her second child. Her death is symbolic of the end of an era. With Ruth is a new beginning. The ingredients are corn, bread, harvest.

The Book of Ruth is in the middle of the historical books of the Bible. It depicts a rural scene and a love story. Amid all the strife and struggle it offers a peaceful little interlude.

The First Kings: Saul, David, Solomon

The rise and fall of a kingdom

SAUL AND DAVID

Samuel received the divine command to seek out and appoint a king. He met Saul, a man who stood head and shoulders above his fellows, when the latter was searching for his father's asses. Samuel recognised him as the appointed one, invited him to a feast, and anointed him.

Saul fought many battles with the enemies of the Israelites but he disobeyed the Lord's commands and worshipped false gods. He had therefore to be replaced and the Lord instructed Samuel to seek a successor from among the children of Jesse, the grandson of Ruth. From Jesse's sons Samuel recognised David as the future king but the appointment was not immediate. Of Saul we learn that he suffered from black moods, that an evil spirit troubled him. He was advised to seek someone to play the harp to him. The choice fell on David but the king knew nothing about David's future rule. David's playing soothed him. He became fond of the boy and made him his armour-bearer.

It was a time of war with the Philistines. Before one of the threatened battles, the Philistine champion, Goliath, came forward and challenged the Israelites to send someone against him in single combat. Only David volunteered. He was discouraged by the king but insisted. He boasted that he had killed a bear and a lion with his bare hands to save a lamb of his father's flocks, and that he was not afraid of Goliath. Saul offered him his armour but David would not take it. With a stone from a sling David despatched Goliath by hitting him in the middle of the forehead.

Jonathan, the son of Saul, became great friends with David and gave him his armour. David became very popular with the people and Saul was jealous.

Several times Saul tried to kill David but failed. David fled to the desert. Several times Saul was at the mercy of David but was spared. Once David took Saul's cup and spear while the latter was sleeping, then showed them to the people in witness of the fact that he could have killed Saul had he wished.

The whole period of Saul's reign was one of war with the various enemies. In many cases Saul was victorious. Some enemies he spared when he should have annihilated them, e.g., the Amalekites. Eventually, he was defeated in battle and killed himself. Jonathan fell at the same time.

The news of their death was brought to David who was very grieved. The kingdom was now divided. David became king of Judah, the southern part of the country. A son of Saul's became king of the other part which retained the name Israel. He, however, was killed and David became king of both Israel and Judah. David made his centre at Jerusalem where he built a palace for himself on Mount Zion and made preparations for building a temple.

But David, too, had his weaknesses and failings. He fell in love with a woman called Bathsheba who was already married. He arranged that her husband should be put in the front line of battle where he would get killed. The arrangement succeeded. The man died and David married the widow.

He ordered the population to be counted but the mere counting without thought of welfare was not approved by the Lord and the people also resented the interference.

David had many struggles to establish the kingdom and many sorrows. One of the things which caused him great distress was that Absalom, his son, led a revolt against him. A battle ensued and as Absalom fled, his hair became entangled in a tree and he remained hanging there. One of David's captains found him and shot him. When the time of his death approached, David appointed Solomon, whose mother was Bathsheba, to be king after him. He was buried on Mount Zion.

NOTES

With the kings comes a much stronger personal element into events. The Psalms and the Song of Solomon are evidence of this.

Now the person is speaking rather than the divine through the person.

Saul represents a transition from divinely led humanity to independent individualities. He was sometimes inspired, sometimes not. He was an aggressive character, a quality well fitted to fighting enemies, but not to guiding a people. He is described as tall, a picture to show that he was still in contact with old forces. In certain moods he became a prophet but this was not an ego activity.

His task was to root out the old decadent clairvoyance which was still prevalent among the peoples surrounding him but he was not sufficiently capable. He suffered from too many human failings: jealousy, anxiety.

David was a different character altogether. His shepherd origin is symbolic. He was one of the *caring*. Saul had sons to succeed him but another line was chosen which would be suitable for the coming Messiah. For David there was a period of preparation. His story begins in Bethlehem, peacefully, then moves to the court before he became king. He was more mature than Saul but he also had weaknesses. He did not fight so many wars but extended the kingdom by pacts.

Saul became king about the year 1020 B.C., David in the year 1000 B.C.

Saul, head and shoulders above his fellows

This should not necessarily be understood in the physical sense. It could signify the extension of the etheric which was not yet in harmony with the physical.

He worshipped other gods

From time to time he was seduced by the beliefs and religious practices of other peoples.

Black moods

He was not in possession of himself. The playing on the harp restored him. David seems to have played the same role as that of Orpheus in Greek mythology.

Goliath

The giant represents old atavistic forces. David has a thinking consciousness. His stone hit Goliath in the middle of the forehead, the seat of the eye of old clairvoyant vision. Overcoming lion and bear means overcoming his own lower instincts.

David's friendship with Jonathan

David refused Saul's armour but accepted Jonathan's. Jonathan was in the new stream. The relationship is an example of friendship which no longer depends on the blood. It is particularly significant in view of Saul's enmity.

Saul's jealousy

The various intrigues show the growing use of the intellect.

David flees to the desert

The experience in the wilderness means finding oneself. This may be real or symbolic, or both in David's case.

Saul is spared

Twice David had the opportunity of killing Saul. Twice he declined, showing that he was sufficiently mature not to retaliate. He even honours Saul after his death. He foreshadows Christ's message: "Love your enemies, bless them that curse you." Spear and cup are symbolic. The spear can be taken as the light of the spirit and the cup is that which signifies receptivity of soul.

Saul spares the Amalekites

Saul failed to fulfil his mission of destroying the old forces, which were being used for evil. When he takes their treasures, it signifies taking part in their practices.

David becomes king of Judah and Israel

This is in recognition of his qualities. Saul's son was not a fit person to rule.

Bathsheba

David was guilty of an immoral act yet Bathsheba became the mother of Solomon. It is a strange turn of fate.

The census

Counting heads in an abstract sense was something strange at that time. It was a quantitative exercise and not qualitative. It upset the people. The time was not ripe for that sort of intellectual thinking.

Absalom's revolt

This represents a throwback to the old ways. Old forces die hard.

David's grave

Over David's grave was supposedly the house where Christ held the Last Supper.

THE PSALMS

A great many of the Psalms were written by David. A few are attributed to Moses and some to the children of Korah. From their content we can see a certain ego development.

Moses belonged to the old world, that of divine revelation. This comes to expression in such Psalms as 90 and 91

The Psalms written by David have a much more personal character and embrace a variety of themes. Some are concerned with Saul and Jonathan; some are prayers for help—3, 22, 54 to 64, 130. Some are connected with special circumstances, e.g., after the affair with Bathsheba, Psalm 51. Some are outpourings of praise, of the Lord or of nature. Only a person who feels his independence could be objective in these matters.

Personal feeling also comes to expression in the Psalms for the sons of Korah, 42, 44–49.

Although Solomon was not the next in line, he was appointed king as being the most suitable. At his request, God gave him wisdom. When two women came to him disputing over a child which both claimed, he ordered the child to be divided. Thereupon one gave up her claim in favour of the other and Solomon judged that the one who yielded must be the real mother.

Solomon became a worldly king. Under him, the Israelites, together with the Phoenicians, travelled over the whole of the known world. Trade with India, Arabia, Africa, brought in precious stones, pearls and gold. He married the daughter of the Egyptian Pharaoh and allied himself with Hiram, King of Tyre. He reorganised the administration for tax gathering. He made the horse popular in the army.

Solomon built cities, forts, aqueducts. Under his direction Jerusalem took on the air of a city. The eastern hill was extended by filling in chasms and the ravine between the hills was filled in. He built himself a magnificent palace and the Lord's Temple. In these matters he was aided by the craftsman, Hiram. The latter cast a sea of molten metal for him and erected two special pillars.

People came in streams to see the wise man (not the divinely inspired priest). Among the many visitors who were very impressed was the Queen of Sheba.

Solomon had many wives and they were the reason why, towards the end of his life, he "lost favour with the Lord."

He reigned for forty years and died in 932 B.C. On his death the kingdom was again divided. The northern part kept the name Israel, with ten tribes ruled by Jeroboam, the son of one of the king's servants. The southern part was ruled by Rehoboam, Solomon's son.

NOTES

Saul, David, Solomon, all move on the human plane more than their predecessors. Saul still struggled with forces outside himself. David struggled too but was more self-possessed. Solomon was the master.

Solomon chooses wisdom

The wisdom that Solomon was given was that of the intellect. The story of the two women disputing illustrates thinking. The judgement does not come through divine revelation.

Trade, administration, building

Solomon's activities were in the practical world. He built a palace for himself and a temple as the outer symbol for the divinity.

The molten sea

This is a symbolic creation. Various metals were melted together to form a vessel, a sort of large bowl. The metals represent the various planets or equally the various soul forces. Fire is used in the melting process, signifying purification. The bowl is the equivalent of the grail. It opens upwards to receive a heavenly content.

The two pillars

These were erected in front of the temple and named Jachim and Boaz. Jachim was constructed to radiate light; Boaz was dark, but phosphorescent. They symbolised birth and death.

Solomon's many wives

He may have had the number of wives quoted but the many wives might also refer to the many cults and forms of worship. Possibly the women came from different cultures and infected Solomon with their beliefs. He suffered the fate of the rich, successful man whose inner development did not keep pace with his outer success. Towards the end of his life he failed.

HISTORICAL NOTE

After Solomon there was disagreement as to the successor and the kingdom was divided. The territory of the ten tribes in the north retained the name of Israel, that of the two tribes in the south, Judah.

Henceforward there was to be no more peace in either country but there was a great stream of spiritual teachers, the prophets. They were not prophets in the strict sense of predicting the future but they tried to guide the people away from the old cults and to prepare for the coming of the Messiah. According to Dr. Steiner they were reincarnated initiates from older cultures; now they came together with a common purpose. They were concerned with the development of human consciousness. They held that suffering strengthened the soul forces. They proclaimed a "dying to become."

The northern kingdom was subject to all sorts of disturbances. Kings gained the throne by murdering their predecessors. Heathen cults flourished. Israel was overcome and totally occupied by the Assyrians in 721 B.C. and ceased to exist. All people of cultural value were deported to Assyria and Medea; people of other lands were brought in. In the far north the inhabitants became known as Galileans; in the centre as Samaritans. The ten tribes disappeared.

In Judah there was relative quiet for a while and the dynasty was orderly. There was a feeling that a descendant of David would be the Messiah. Judah remained free until after the reign of Hezekiah (715–686 B.C.) when it became subject to the Assyrians. At the same time Judah was not immune to negative influences and its people suffered.

The Prophets: Elijah, Elisha, Jonah, Isaiah

The call to repentance. The coming Messiah

ELIJAH

There was often strife between Israel and Judah and also between Israel and its northern neighbour, Syria. Within each kingdom there were disputes over religion.

A man called Ahab had come to rule in Israel. He married a Tyrian princess, Jezebel, who introduced the Baal cult into her adopted country. The Lord was displeased and instructed Elijah, the Man of God, to tell Ahab that there would be neither dew nor rain in the land until further notice. Having announced this, Elijah was to journey to a certain brook where he would be fed by ravens. When the brook dried up, he was instructed to seek out a certain widow who would care for him. He found the widow and asked for food but she answered that her store of meal and oil was insufficient. He asked her to make a cake nevertheless and, miraculously, there was always more oil and meal in the containers. The widow's son fell ill and was apparently dead but Elijah resurrected him.

Elijah returned to Ahab and a contest was staged with the priests of Baal. Elijah was victorious and all the priests were slain. This made Jezebel very angry and she swore revenge. Elijah looked into the distance and predicted rain.

He then fled into the wilderness where an angel hovered over him. The Lord told him to go to Mount Horeb and there he experienced fire, earthquake and whirlwind, but he did not hear the voice of the Lord in them. Instead he heard a still, small voice within himself. He was told to go to Damascus to anoint a new king, to go to Israel to do likewise. He was also to denounce malpractices and to appoint Elisha as his successor.

When Elijah was not speaking in the name of the Lord, he took on another appearance and another name. Then he was known as Naboth. Not many people knew this but among those who did was Jezebel.

Naboth had a vineyard next to Ahab's palace and the king wanted it. Naboth would not sell it. Jezebel, however, arranged for him to be killed, then told the king that since Naboth was dead, he could take possession.

Ahab went into the vineyard but a terrible shock awaited him. Naboth-Elijah appeared to him in a vision and proclaimed his end. He then realised with horror what had happened and was filled with remorse. A little later he was killed in battle.

When the time came for Elijah to leave the earthly sphere, he and Elisha were standing by the River Jordan. Elijah asked Elisha what he could do for him before being taken away and Elisha asked that his spirit might descend on him. As they talked a chariot of fire and horses of fire appeared and parted them; Elijah went up by a whirlwind into heaven. Elisha had a vision of Elijah's mantle falling to earth which he acquired. The people who experienced this event knelt down before Elisha saying that now the spirit of Elijah rested on him.

NOTES

With Elijah there is a turning point in the experience of the divinity. Moses had heard the voice of God in the elements; Elijah hears it within. Looking on the Christ event as a descent from the cosmic spheres, we now see that the divine voice is making itself heard within the soul. Elijah is not a prophet in the sense of foretelling future events but he foreshadows the coming Messiah.

The northern kingdom of Israel was degenerate and was finally overrun by the Assyrians. It was left to the people of Judah, the Jews, to tread the narrow path although they also strayed from time to time.

Elijah is an enigmatic character. He is referred to as a "Man of God"; an angel often overshadows him. He appears here and there, then disappears. Sometimes he is helping the oppressed; sometimes combatting evildoers. He is fed by ravens at one end of the country and the next recorded episode (with the widow) takes place at the other.

The problem of his personality is considerably clarified if we accept Dr. Steiner's indication that Elijah and Naboth were one. This fact has been inserted into the narrative above. It clarifies the Bible story.

It would seem that Elijah had some connection with the Mithras Mysteries.

Elijah denounces Ahab

Ahab had allowed the worship of Baal to be introduced and was therefore at fault. Elijah announced a drought which could be real but more likely represented spiritual thirst.

Elijah journeys to the wilderness and is fed by ravens

This represents a soul experience. The wilderness experience is a step on the path to knowledge. In the Mithras Mysteries the Raven (Corax) symbolised the first degree of initiation, a person capable of receiving divine messages, a messenger. Perhaps Elijah himself was at the stage of the "Raven."

The widow

The widow is the one who is left lonely, having to find in herself new forces. In this sense Elijah is a widow. Resurrecting her son means self-renewal. Meal and oil are spiritual sustenance. It is another experience of the soul.

Contest with the priests of Baal

New forces overcome the old. Fire from heaven is ego-consciousness. If taken as a physical demonstration, it must have awakened the Israelites to their true faith.

Mount Horeb (Sinai)

Four centuries have passed since Moses was here. At that time the divinity spoke in the elements; now the scene is the human soul; Elijah hears the still, small voice within.

Appointment of new kings in Israel and Syria

Like the two giants in the fairy story, they will destroy one another.

Naboth and the vineyard

Jezebel succeeds in destroying the physical body of Naboth-Elijah.

Ahab in the vineyard

Ahab did not realise until now that Naboth and Elijah were the same personality. He was devastated, particularly also because he realised his doom and that of his house and kingdom.

Elijah's departure

According to Dr. Steiner the request made by Elisha should read: I would that your spirit continues to live within me like a second ego.

The chariot of fire

Elijah underwent many experiences which can be interpreted as stages of initiation. At the end of his life he had transformed and purified his being. This is perceived by Elisha's spiritual vision as a chariot of fire. Elijah had represented and furthered the Israelite impulse. He was carrying it therefore in his soul, the chariot. The fact that fire is mentioned points to a further development or a further stage of initiation. This is "Courier of the Sun" (Heliodromus). The Mithras cult was concerned with an experience of the conquering spirit of the sun, the future Christ. Elisha was aware of Elijah's attainments.

"My father, my father, the chariot of Israel and the horsemen thereof"

Elisha's words, as they stand, do not make much sense. "My father" could be taken in the sense of mentor but more likely it refers to the highest degree of initiation in the Mithras cult (Pater). "The chariot of Israel and the horsemen thereof" signifies

fies that Elijah incorporated the essence of the Hebrew people and furthered it (the horsemen) and his soul was transformed accordingly.

ELISHA

Elisha continued the work of Elijah. He also had power over water and he performed many miracles. He "divided the waters."

He was at Jericho and was asked to purify the water which was undrinkable. He went to the spring, threw salt in it and the waters were healed. Once children mocked him calling out "bald head," but bears came out of the woods and devoured them.

The kings of Israel, Judah and Edom combined to fight the Moabites but found themselves in a land suffering from drought. Elisha told them to dig trenches which became filled with water. When the Moabites saw it, they thought that it was the blood of their opponents who had mutually quarrelled. They attacked but were defeated.

A creditor demanded payment from the widow of a prophet and threatened to take her two sons as slaves in lieu. Elisha asked what she had in the house and she answered "a pot of oil." He told her to borrow all the vessels that she could from her neighbours and to pour the oil into them. They were all filled. Then he told her to sell the oil to pay her debts and to live on the further proceeds.

A Shunamite woman provided Elisha with hospitality. He prophesied that she would have a son in spite of her husband's old age. She doubted but it came true. One day the child was out in the field and developed a headache, was taken home and died. Elisha restored him with the warmth of his own body.

There was a shortage of food and Elisha's disciples made a soup of herbs, the nature of which they did not know. When they tasted it, they found it impossible to drink and poisonous. Elisha threw meal into it and the soup became wholesome. On another occasion he fed a hundred men with twenty loaves.

Naaman, captain of the King of Syria's guard, came to Elisha to be healed of his leprosy. Elisha told him to bathe seven times in the River Jordan. Naaman thought that he was being ridiculed and became angry. He was finally persuaded, and cured. He offered a reward. Elisha would not take it but Elisha's servant asked secretly for payment which Naaman gave him. But Elisha knew and when the servant returned, the leprosy was visited on him.

Elisha's disciples wanted to live by the River Jordan. They were cutting down trees when one of them dropped his axe into the water. He was distressed because it was borrowed but Elisha threw in a twig and the axe floated to the surface.

When an enemy host came to take him, Elisha prayed that they should be smitten by blindness, then they were led away.

Elisha became ill and the King of Israel, Joash, came to see him and addressed him: "O my father, my father, the chariot of Israel and the horsemen thereof." Elisha told him to string a bow with an arrow; he put his hands on the king's hands and told him to shoot. "That," he said, "is the arrow of the Lord's deliverance."

He was buried in a sepulchre and when a dead man was thrown in and touched his bones, the dead man revived.

NOTES

From his pupils Elijah chose the one most suited to carry on his work. There are many similarities in the two lives. Elisha divides the waters. He purifies the spring at Jericho. He has the same spiritual powers as Elijah. The waters are often a picture of the etheric world, the world of the life forces. Elisha gives a new impulse to a new spiritual life.

Bald head

Thinkers and bald heads are often associated although for no particular reason. In this case bald head is symbolic of the trend towards intellectual thinking.

The water in the ditches appears as blood

In the changing nature of man the etheric becomes more closely connected with the physical and the ego becomes more active within the body. The Moabites had clairvoyant vision and saw this change in their enemies as a weakness.

The widow in debt

Like Elijah, Elisha experiences his own soul as a widow. The perpetual stream of oil is the inexhaustible spiritual.

The Shunamite woman

The death of her son from a headache signifies that intellectual head forces lead to a deadness of soul. These forces must be united with human warmth, with warmth of heart.

The bitter soup

Hard times are coming. Elisha provides spiritual sustenance.

Naaman's leprosy—The floating axe—Blindness of the enemy

These are all symbolic of spiritual rejuvenation or the necessity for it.

"My father, my father, the chariot of Israel and the horsemen thereof"

The king speaks the same words to Elisha as Elisha had spoken to Elijah. It is to be inferred that both were high initiates in the Mithras Mysteries.

Shooting the arrow

Elisha invokes the king to continue the struggle. The arrow represents the force of the ego.

A dead man touches Elisha's bones and revives

Elisha's influence continues. It is a source of revivification.

JONAH

The Lord told Jonah to go to Nineveh (Assyria) to preach against the evil taking place there. Jonah was reluctant and tried to escape by taking a ship to Tarshish. A great storm arose but Jonah slept. The ship's master told him to call on his god to save them. The company cast lots to see who was at fault and the lot fell on Jonah. He was cast overboard and the storm abated. He was swallowed by a whale and after three days and nights was deposited on shore. He was told again to go to Nineveh. This time he went and after his warnings, the people repented. He became angry and felt that the Lord had let him down. He sat outside the city. A gourd protected him from the sun but a worm ate it. The Lord explained that just as Jonah had had pity for the gourd, so he had pity for Nineveh.

NOTES

The Book of Jonah is short and the narrative appears to lack a conclusion. Jonah himself appears in history just before the Assyrians occupy the northern kingdom. He is sent to preach to them and they repent. At the end of the story is the enigmatic episode with the gourd and the conversation with God. Yet a few years later the Assyrians destroyed Israel and scattered its people.

Jonah tries to avoid the Lord's command

This is not surprising in view of the situation. Assyria was a threat and there was enmity between that country and Israel. To send Jonah there was like asking him to put his head in the lion's mouth. However, he had a mission and fate arranged that he had to realise his destiny.

The storm

Was this a storm in Jonah's soul or a physical one? Perhaps it was both. The outer storm may have provoked the inner one and the visionary experience of the whale episode.

In the belly of the whale

The picture is of an initiation. It is equal to the three days' temple sleep of the Egyptians and other cultures.

Nineveh repents

The effect of Jonah's preaching was that the Assyrians paused for reflection. Maybe the moral strength shown by Jonah impressed them and they might well have asked whence it came. If the strength were due to Israelite secret knowledge, it would be an incentive to conquer Israel to acquire it.

The gourd

In the picture of the gourd growing over his head, Jonah has the feeling of shelter within his race. The gourd withers and dies by a divine act and Jonah is distressed. He realises that the destruction of his people through the Assyrians is imminent but that it is part of the divine plan. He is angry but the Lord is also apparently not happy at the destruction to come.

ISAIAH

Isaiah called upon the people to give up their wicked ways and predicted that dreadful calamities would overtake them if they did not. In the year that King Uzziah died, Isaiah had a vision of God's throne and angelic beings around it. He then prophesied not only how the many surrounding peoples engaged in false worship would be destroyed but also how Judah would eventually triumph and fulfill its mission in receiving the Christ.

The ruling king at this period was Hezekiah who destroyed the cultic symbols and also the altars of the false gods. He ordered the priests to sanctify and purify the house of the Lord.

The country was threatened from the north but Isaiah prophesied that a remnant of Judah would remain faithful and that the city of Jerusalem would not fall to the invaders.

In the fourteenth year of Hezekiah's reign, the Assyrians, under their king, Sennacherib, laid seige to Jerusalem, but in the night the Angel of the Lord swept over their armies and they were destroyed. Sennacherib returned to his own country where he was murdered by his sons.

Some time later Hezekiah fell ill and Isaiah thought that he would die. Then the word of the Lord came to him to tell him to tell Hezekiah that his life would be prolonged. As a sign the shadow of the sundial turned back. In his sickness Hezekiah had learned much and now he amassed new riches and completed many new works.

The news of the destruction of the Assyrian army and the wonderful recovery of Hezekiah spread and attracted visitors. Among them came the Babylonians and Hezekiah showed them all his treasures. When Isaiah learned of this, he was very angry.

NOTES

Isaiah was the great prophet-teacher who was particularly engaged in the struggle against the effects of old atavistic clairvoyance. He inspired King Hezekiah to destroy the old cults. During Hezekiah's reign the country prospered.

The vision of God's throne

This revelation gave Isaiah a new impulse. The year was 740 B.C.

Hezekiah destroys the symbols

These inspired old clairvoyance. They had to be destroyed because inner development was now essential.

The destruction of the Assyrian armies

Two explanations are possible. Perhaps a physical destruction took place through the presence of volcanic gases. Symbolically, the Assyrians had a presentiment of stronger forces and the experience was spiritual. Byron has written a marvelous poem on the episode.

Hezekiah's illness

Hezekiah experienced an initiation. He gathered new insight and learned more of his destiny. It also affected Isaiah who realised his further task and what he had to announce for the future. It was a demonstration of death and resurrection, a foreshadowing of the Messiah.

The visit of the Babylonians

Delegates came to see Hezekiah and he told them of his spiritual experiences (treasures). The Babylonians had the feeling that some supernatural force that they would like to acquire was at work in Judah. Unwittingly, Hezekiah had brought destruction on his people.

Isaiah was cross

He realised the unpleasant consequences. In time the Babylonians would take the Jews into captivity.

THE BAAL CULT—SACRIFICE OF THE FIRSTBORN

There is an intimate spiritual connection between mother, father and child. A soul descends from the spiritual world into the loving surroundings of the parents. In the Bible record great personalities are consciously expected, announced by higher beings. The object of the Baal cult was to create chaos in the normal workings of destiny.

The Babylonian Captivity: Jeremiah, Ezekiel, Daniel

The dark hour before the dawn

JEREMIAH

Jeremiah was called upon by the Lord to be his mouthpiece. He was told that people would fight against him but that they would not prevail. He was instructed to proclaim to the children of Israel that they had forgotten the Lord God and were doing all manner of wicked things. Both Israel and Judah had forsaken the right paths, should repent and turn again to the ways of the Lord.

Jeremiah complained that the wicked were prospering and that he was being cursed by everyone, but the Lord promised him help and deliverance. He was told to foretell the destruction of Judah and Jerusalem because of the wicked ways of their peoples.

One of the priests got tired of Jeremiah's preaching and had him put in the stocks for the night, but, being released, he continued to preach and also predicted that the priest would be taken captive to Babylon and die there.

Repeatedly Jeremiah complained to the Lord about his hard fate and the way people treated him, but he continued to prophesy. He warned against false prophets and foretold the coming of Christ.

He predicted that the Jews would be in Babylonian captivity for seventy years but that Babylon would eventually be destroyed. Once again he was arrested but defended himself as the spokesman of the Lord. Some believed him and he was released. Some Jews had already been deported and he wrote a letter of encouragement to them saying they would be freed in the course of time.

During the reign of Zedekiah Jeremiah was again imprisoned for preaching destruction. Released again, he still continued to prophesy. He told Zedekiah that he would be overthrown by Nebuchadnezzar, taken captive and that Jerusalem would be destroyed. Jeremiah's secretary, Baruch, wrote these things down and then read the script to the people. It was also read to the king who tore up the manuscript and burnt it, whereupon Baruch wrote it all down again.

Jeremiah tried to leave the city but was again arrested and imprisoned. While he was in prison, the Babylonians captured the city. Their king ordered Jeremiah to be set free and to be allowed to live where he wished. Some of the Jews then sought Jeremiah's advice as to where they should go. He told them to stay where they were but they disregarded this and went to Egypt, taking him with them. In Egypt he died and legends say that he was stoned to death by his own people.

NOTES

After Hezekiah's death there was retrogression under Manasseh. Following him, under his grandson, Josiah, there was reform again. Josiah came to the throne as an eight-year-old boy in 640 B.C. The Jews at that time were subject to the Assyrians, whose power was declining, but who were now allied with the Egyptians in their common struggle against the Babylonians. Josiah made a bid for independence but was defeated and killed by the Egyptians at the battle of Megiddo, 609 B.C. In the meantime Babylon was becoming the dominant power. Assyria and Judah became part of the Babylonian empire. All sorts of strange and evil cults were introduced. About the year 579 B.C. many elite Jews were deported to Babylon. In 586 B.C. Jerusalem was captured and destroyed by Nebuchadnezzar and all Jews were taken into captivity except those who escaped to Egypt.

Jeremiah the prophet lived during this period. He first appears in 626 B.C. when he was about twenty years old. He expresses the woe and sorrow of the Jewish people. He experienced the black hour of Jewish history and encouraged the people to bear their burdens patiently. He made himself unpopular by advocating cooperation with the conquerors.

The Jews in exile

The deportation of the Jews to Babylon meant the acquisition by the Babylonians of both slave labour and knowledge. It will be noted that Jeremiah was set free. Nebuchadnezzar had a similar idea to that which the Romans later achieved, namely, a Pantheon.

One effect of the captivity was to strengthen Jewish culture. It was in the Babylonian exile that the idea af a synagogue took root and a group of writers appeared to write down the Jewish beliefs. They probably worked with Babylonian experts. They had no temple.

More important was the fact that the Jews came into contact with the reincarnated Zarathustra who was teaching in the mystery centres of Babylon and whose later connection with the Christ being is explained in Rudolf Steiner's Christology. Besides the Jewish prophets, Pythagoras was also a pupil of Zarathustra.

The Babylonians were conquered by the Persians under Cyrus II in 537 B.C. but the Persians did not suppress other religions. Cyrus was an enlightened ruler. He sent 30,000 Jews back to Jerusalem to rebuild the temple.

EZEKIEL

Ezekiel was a priest and was among the first batch of Jews to be taken from Judah to Babylon. Standing by a river one day he had a vision of a whirlwind, with fire in the midst of it and in it he saw forms as of four living creatures, man, lion, ox and eagle. Over their heads was the firmament and over that a throne on which was seated a shining figure. The brightness around the throne was like a rainbow.

A voice addressed him as "Son of Man" and ordered him to denounce the wickedness of the people and to call upon them to change their ways. At the same time he was told to explain that a remnant of the Israelites would be saved from destruction. He foretold the great troubles which would beset not only the Israelites who did wrong but all the surrounding peoples.

On another occasion he had a vision of a valley of dry bones and was commanded by the Lord to prophesy that they would become living human beings. This was a symbol of the resurrection of the house of Israel.

Ezekiel set out the rules by which priests and people should live.

NOTES

Ezekiel admonished, denounced and comforted his people. Like Jeremiah he predicted that catastrophes and downfall would precede a change. He was taken to Babylon around 597 B.C.

Vision of the whirlwind and the four creatures

Ezekiel sees wheels turning—possibly an experience of his own soul-spiritual organs of perception. He sees the figure of Christ among the hierarchies and a picture of ideal man in the four creatures.

Son of Man

This signifies a condition of consciousness (Spirit Self) that Ezekiel has reached.

The valley of dry bones

The symbolism is pointed out in the story. The spirit of Israel will live. It is a picture of death and resurrection.

DANIEL

Among the captives taken to Babylon was a boy who proved to have remarkable gifts. This was Daniel.

With several others he was chosen to be brought up at the king's court. They were given new names. They were to eat the king's meat and drink the king's wine. They became friendly with the master of the king's household and said that they wanted their own diet. The master thought that they would become ill and that he would get the blame but they persuaded him to give them a ten-day trial period. To his surprise they looked better at the end of the ten days than did the other boys at the court.

The king had a dream but could not remember it. His wise men could not help. Daniel offered his services, saying that there was a God in heaven who would reveal secrets to him. He then described an image seen by Nebuchadnezzar in his dream. It was a statue with a head of gold, breast and arms of silver, belly and thighs of brass, legs of iron, feet of a mixture of iron and clay. A stone smashed the feet, the rest collapsed, broke up and was carried away by the wind. The stone grew to a mountain and filled the earth. Then Daniel explained: "The head of gold means that you are a mighty king. After you will be a kingdom less powerful, then a third, less still, and the fourth shall break in pieces. As the feet of clay crumbled, so will this kingdom be divided. Part of it will be strong and part weak, but it will be dispersed. Then a new kingdom will arise which will last for ever."

The king bowed to Daniel and made him a great man. At Daniel's request, his immediate companions, Shadrach, Meshach and Abednego, were also advanced.

King Nebuchadnezzar set up a golden image and ordered it to be worshipped at the sound of certain music, on pain of being thrown into a fiery furnace if disobedient. Daniel's companions refused, were cast into the fire but they received no harm and a fourth figure was seen among them. They were brought forth, testified to their god and Nebuchadnezzar decreed that henceforth nothing should be spoken against this god.

The king had a second dream. He saw a tree growing from earth to heaven with enough fruit on it to feed every thing and every one. A holy one came down and cried, "Cut down the tree, cut off the branches, shake off the leaves, scatter the fruit but leave the stump. Man's heart shall be changed to that of a beast." Daniel gave the interpretation that the king was the great tree. Enemies would destroy most of his kingdom but a foundation would remain. The king would live like an animal for a time but become strong again and realise who was the true god.

When Nebuchadnezzar died, Belshazzar succeeded him. Belshazzar gave a great feast, using the goblets from the temple at Jerusalem and extolling the virtues of the heathen gods. Then came a hand which wrote a message on the wall which noone could interpret but Daniel. He explained it to the king: "By the order of God your kingdom shall be no more. You have been found wanting. Your kingdom will be divided between the Medes and the Persians." Daniel was honoured for his interpretation. The king died that same night.

Darius, the Median, took the kingdom and appointed Daniel to a high position. This displeased others and they tried to snare him with the result that he was thrown into a lion's den. The king was worried but no lion touched Daniel. He was released, explained how his god had sent an angel to shut the lions' mouths. The accusers were thrown into the den and were devoured.

Daniel had other visions. He saw distorted figures of four beasts. He saw a ram with two horns and a he-goat with one, and the angel Gabriel explained this latter vision to him, i.e., Greece would overcome Persia.

He had a further vision of a being of dazzling appearance who told him of all the troubles which would beset the world and how Persia would be overcome by Greece, and Greece by Rome. There would be great destruction. By the side of this figure stood another and Daniel was given to understand that this was the Archangel Michael.

Finally he saw a man clothed in linen standing on the far side of a river and the Archangel Michael on the near side. He overheard Michael asking about the time of fulfillment and was told it would be in due season.

NOTES

Judah was conquered by the Babylonians and its people were taken into captivity. The background to events was that they should no longer think of Jerusalem as a physical thing but should look towards the coming of the Messiah and the New Jerusalem.

Daniel had much in common with Joseph. He was a great personality and stood above nationality. He brought new impulses into Babylonian life. He was retained as adviser even when the Persians invaded. It is possible that he had already visited the Persian court before the invasion.

He had great personal power. What could have been his martyrdom, he overcame through superior spiritual power.

The boys were given new names, the king's meat etc.

It was intended that they should be taught Babylonian ways and that they should be initiated into Babylonian mysteries. The feeding of special foods is a sign that they were being schooled in a particular direction but they preferred their own (Nazarite) way. When it is said that they became more beautiful and clever than their companions, it signifies that their spiritual development was greater.

The king's first dream

Daniel interpreted this on one level but there is another. It could have been an experience of the development of humanity. Once there was a golden age when humans and gods walked side by side. Then there were less golden ages and human consciousness turned gradually to the earth. People developed independent ego forces.

The fiery furnace

The Jews must prove their worth. The three companions are overshadowed by one who was like the son of God. Is this Daniel? Or a guardian angel? It is an imaginative picture of a trial in which the spirit is victorious.

The king's second dream

Daniel gives an interpretation relating to the king but it could also signify the disappearance of old clairvoyant capacities. This would bring about a low level of understanding until the new faculties of thinking were developed.

Balshazzar's feast

The biblical and historic records are somewhat at variance. The historical Belshazzar lived at a later period. The immediate successor to Nebuchadnezzar was Evil-Merodach who ruled from 562 to 560 B.C. It is possible that Belshazzar was his second name.

The writing on the wall

This signifies the end of Babylon and the old cults and forces.

Belshazzar dies

The Bible gives Darius as the next king. The historical Darius (several of them) lived later. The explanation may be the same as with Belshazzar.

Daniel and his companions are promoted

The Babylonians recognise their wisdom and seek to attain it.

The lion's den

There are various ways of understanding this episode. It could be a picture of Daniel overcoming his own lower nature, as with Samson. It could show the conquest of spirit over danger and threatened martyrdom, or the protection afforded by higher powers.

The four beasts

These are creatures of evil which will seek to influence humanity. The fourth and the most horrible has the countenance of Ahriman, but it will be destroyed and God's kingdom established.

The ram and the he-goat

The Angel Gabriel gives Daniel the interpretation: the Medes and Persians will be overcome by the Greeks. Symbolically, ancient clairvoyance will be overtaken by the intellect but cold intellectual understanding is incapable of comprehending holy things.

The vision of Christ

Daniel learns of things to come, materialism and the destruction of the temple. Symbolically, selfish egoism will prevail for a while but Daniel should not despair.

The two figures by the river

One is Christ and the other Michael. The Archangel points the way.

HISTORICAL NOTE

In the Biblical record Daniel is adviser to four kings: Nebuchadnezzar, Belshazzar, Darius and Cyrus. Historically the sequence of kings from Nebuchadnezzar is as follows (not all dates are verifiable):

Babylonian kings: reigned

B.C.	605–562	Nebuchadnezzar
	562–560	Awil-Marduk, also known as Evil-Merodach
	559–556	Nergal-Shar-Usur
	555–539	Nabonidus and his vice-regent, Belshazzar

Persian kings: reigned

B.C.	539–529	Cyrus II, the Great
	529–522	Cambyses II
	522–486	Darius I, the Great

It is to be assumed that Daniel was adviser to them all. The discrepancy could be explained in various ways. Possibly the less famous names were left out of the record. The kings may have had second names. Some genuine confusion could have arisen among the writers. The kings referred to in the Bible are: Nebuchadnezzar II, Belshazzar, Darius I and Cyrus II.

The following is the sequence of rulers after Darius I:

B.C.	486–465	Xerxes I
	465–425	Artaxerxes I
	425–424	Xerxes II
	423–404	Darius II
	404–359	Artaxerxes II
	359–338	Artaxerxes III
	337–330	Darius III

With the conquests of Alexander, Judah came under the rule of Macedonian kings, first the dynasty of the Ptolomies, then the Seleucids. Rome intervened in 63 B.C. Herod became king under Roman rule in 37 B.C.

The Return to Jerusalem: Ezra, Nehemiah

Reform and reconstruction

EZRA

Cyrus was well disposed towards the Jews and allowed those who wished to do so to return to their own country. He gave back to them the temple treasures which Nebuchadnezzar had taken.

Other people put difficulties in their way. The local officials were annoyed and so were adherents of other religions. The objectors conspired together and wrote to Ahasuerus who had succeeded to the throne, and then to his successor (Artaxerxes). They suggested that the Jews would become too powerful and would possibly cause disturbance and rebellion. An edict was issued forbidding further building. The situation changed when Darius became king. Application was made to him on behalf of the Jews and he ordered the records to be searched. The original edict given by Cyrus was found. Darius confirmed that the work should go ahead. He gave material assistance and decreed that anyone who tried to hinder the building should be punished.

Later in the narrative it is recorded that Artaxerxes also decreed that all Jews who wished might return to their own land. He appointed Ezra, "the priest, a scribe of the law of the God of heaven," to be their leader.

NOTES

In the order of books in the Old Testament, Ezra (and Nehemiah) follow immediately after the Chronicles but in historical sequence the stories are better placed here.

The text as it appears in the Bible presents a problem. Ahasuerus can be identified as Xerxes I who reigned 486–465 B.C. His successor is named as Artaxerxes, presumably Artaxerxes Longimanus. The story indicates that Artaxerxes was both help and hindrance to the Jews. However, dates and names do not coincide with known historical facts. There is no real explanation.

Artaxerxes I ruled 465–425 B.C. Ezra returned to Jerusalem in 458. He was a literary scholar and an expert on the law. His task was to reform religious life and to explain the Mosaic law. Besides his direct reforms Ezra collected and edited the old writings which contained the laws. This could only be done by one who had the necessary insight. Ezra probably founded synagogues.

Most of the Jews who had returned in 538 B.C. had been born in Babylon and knew nothing of the old land. Those who remained in Babylon were not happy about developments because they felt that the first exiles did not carry the right impulse.

It is estimated that some 50,000 Jews returned from exile in 538 B.C. When Ezra returned, it was as the king's appointed commissioner.

NEHEMIAH

Artaxerxes had a servant called Nehemiah. One day the servant was bringing him wine when the king noticed that he looked sad and asked him the cause. Nehemiah said that he mourned for Jerusalem. He had heard how the city was falling into ruin and he would like to return to restore it. The king granted his request and also offered assistance in providing material. The king made Nehemiah governor. But the people of other races were not so pleased at seeing the Jews restore the city and they plotted to hinder the work. Nehemiah organized the workers into two groups; one stood on guard while the other worked, but even those who worked also carried a weapon. The walls were rebuilt in fifty-two days and then there was a great celebration.

NOTES

Nehemiah was active in the years 445 –430 B.C. and cooperated with Ezra in making reforms.

THE TWELVE MINOR PROPHETS

The last twelve books of the Old Testament bear the names of the so-called minor prophets. These individuals were active between about the years 800–400 B.C., the period roughly from the destruction of the northern kingdom of Israel to the return of the Jews from Babylonian captivity. With the exception of the book of Jonah, which has more the character of a narrative, they all touch on the same themes: denunciation of evil practices, divine wrath with the promise of forgiveness on repentance, comfort for sufferings endured and the advent of the Messiah.

The Story of Esther

Jews are saved from destruction

ESTHER

King Ahasuerus (Xerxes I) ruled from India to Ethiopia. His capital was at Shushan (Susa). He gave a great feast and wished to show off his wife to all the guests but she refused to appear. He consulted his wise men as to the law and it was decided that she should be dismissed and that he should choose another.

At his court there was a Jew, Mordecai by name, who had brought up his niece since her parents were dead. This girl, Esther, was chosen by the king to be his queen. It was not known that uncle and niece were Jews.

It happened that Mordecai became aware of a plot to murder the king which he disclosed to Esther. She, in turn, warned the king and the plot was foiled.

Also at the court was an ambitious official named Haman who had ingratiated himself with the king and was very much in his favour, so much so, that the king ordered others to bow to him as a sign of respect. Mordecai refused to do this. Haman found out that he was a Jew and devised a way to get rid of him and all other Jews as well.

Haman informed the king that there were people in his realm who had their own laws and disobeyed the king's. He suggested the possibility of revolt and advised that these people be put to death. The king, trusting his adviser, gave him authority to act as he thought best, whereupon Haman published an edict in the king's name declaring that the Jews were to be annihilated. For Mordecai he prepared a special gallows.

When this became known to the queen, she asked Mordecai for advice and he told her to intercede with the king, pointing out that perhaps it was for this very reason that she had become queen.

The queen agreed but did not plead immediately. She invited the king and Haman to come to a banquet which would be prepared for them alone.

One night, in the meantime, the king was restless and could not sleep. He sent for the books of the chronicles in which he discovered that Mordecai had not been rewarded for saving his life.

The next day he asked Haman how a worthy man should be honoured and Haman, thinking the reference was to himself, said that he should be given royal apparel, a crown and the king's horse. The king ordered Haman to take such presents to Mordecai, which he did, but with much discomfort.

When the banquet was held, Esther exposed what Haman had done in the king's name. She pleaded that her people were the proposed victims, thus admitting her nationality. She explained how Haman had given false reports about her race whereupon the king cancelled the edict immediately. Haman was hanged on the gallows he had set up for Mordecai.

The order was given that the Jews were to be left in peace. Mordecai was then given Haman's position and was even further advanced in rank.

NOTES

There is no known historical basis for this story; rather does it belong to the realm of legend. It is still told on festive occasions but for the Jews during their time of dispersal, it must have had a particular significance. It was an encouragement and a confirmation of their mission.

Esther and Mordecai in Shushan

Esther is an orphan. Both are in a foreign land. The facts illustrate the homelessness of the Jews.

Esther becomes queen

Interpreted symbolically, this means that Jewish culture is accorded an important place.

Plot against the king

The king makes no racial discrimination but narrow interests work against him.

The edict to destroy the Jews

Negative forces seek to hold back progressive elements of evolution.

The king reads the records

A symbolic interpretation is that the king recognises the Jewish mission.

Esther exposes Haman. Mordecai is honoured

The tables are turned. Jewish influence predominates. Although Judah was conquered physically, it was victorious spiritually.

NOTE ON SOURCES

It is difficult to compile a comprehensive bibliography since Dr. Steiner's indications are scattered throughout his works. Moreover, in fifty years' study of anthroposophy, the author has absorbed or developed ideas without being able to recall the exact time or place of reference or inspiration.

The evolutionary development of humankind and the earth are described in several of Rudolf Steiner's books or lecture courses: *An Outline of Esoteric Science* (formerly published under the title *Occult Science: An Outline, At the Gates of Spiritual Science, Rosicrucian Esotericism, Universe, Earth and Man*; and *The Gospel of St. John*. The seven days of creation are dealt with in *Genesis* (formerly published under the title *Biblical Secrets of Creation*). Reference to the great characters of the Old Testament are to be found in: *Turning Points of Spiritual History*, the lecture cycle on St. Luke's Gospel (lecture 6), the lectures on the Gospel of St. Mark (lectures 2, 3). Information concerning the Jews in Babylonian captivity is to be found in the lectures on the Gospel of St. Matthew. To appreciate the connections between the Elohim, Jehovah and Christ, a fuller study of Rudolf Steiner's Christology is necessary.

BOOKS BY ROY WILKINSON

Questions and Answers on Rudolf Steiner Education
The Temperaments in Education
The Interpretation of Fairy Tales
The Curriculum of the Rudolf Steiner School
Commonsense Schooling
Rudolf Steiner on Education

Wilkinson Waldorf Curriculum Series:
Teaching English
Teaching Mathematics
Teaching Physics and Chemistry
Teaching Geography
Teaching History I: *Ancient Civilizations, Greece, Rome*
Teaching History II: *Middle Ages, Renaissance to the Second World War*
Old Testament Stories
Commentary on the Old Testament Stories
The Norse Stories and their Significance
Teaching Practical Activities: *Farming, Gardening, Housebuilding*
The Human Being and the Animal World
Plant Study and Geology
Nutrition, Health, and Anthropology
Miscellany: *A Collection of Poems and Plays*
Plays for Puppets

The Origin and Development of Language
The Spiritual Basis of Rudolf Steiner Education

Rudolf Steiner: Aspects of his spiritual world view (3 volumes)
Anthroposophy vol. I: *Rudolf Steiner. Reincarnation and karma. The spiritual nature of the human being. The development of human consciousness.*
Anthroposophy vol. II: *Evolution of the world and humanity. Relationships between the living and the dead. Forces of evil. The modern path of initiation.*
Anthroposophy vol. III: *Life between death and rebirth. The spiritual hierarchies. The philosophical approach to the spirit. The mission of Christ.*

May be ordered from: Rudolf Steiner College Bookstore
9200 Fair Oaks Boulevard
Fair Oaks, CA 95628, USA
Tel: (916) 961-8729 — Fax: (916) 961-3032